Overcoming Common Problems Series

Selected titles

A full list of titles is available from Sheldon Press,
36 Causton Street, London SW1P 4ST and on our website at
www.sheldonpress.co.uk

Overcoming Common Problems Series

Overcoming Common Problems Series

Overcoming Common Problems

Coping with Manipulation

When others blame you for their feelings

DR WINDY DRYDEN

First published in Great Britain in 2011

Sheldon Press
36 Causton Street
London SW1P 4ST
www.sheldonpress.co.uk

British Library Cataloguing-in-Publication Data
A catalogue record for this book is available from the British Library

ISBN 978-1-84709-135-2

Typeset by Caroline Waldron, Wirral, Cheshire
First printed in Great Britain by Ashford Colour Press
Subsequently digitally printed in Great Britain

Produced on paper from sustainable forests

Contents

1

People feel the way they believe

The principle of emotional responsibility

Introduction

This book focuses on the common situation when someone blames you for the way that he or she feels. When this happens the person may say only that you caused those feelings or additionally he or she may depreciate you for causing them. In this book, I will lump both together. Here are some examples of what people may say to you when they blame you or hold you responsible for upsetting them, depending on the nature of their feelings.

- 'You have upset me.'
- 'You frighten me.'
- 'You make me depressed.'
- 'You have guilt-tripped me.'
- 'You have made me so ashamed to be a member of this family.'
- 'You make me so angry when you won't listen to me.'
- 'You have really hurt my feelings.'
- 'You made me mad with jealousy when you flirted with that man at the party.'
- 'You like to make me really envious of you, don't you?'

In Chapter 3, I will discuss the reasons why people blame you for the way that they feel. But first, in this chapter, I will outline the principle of emotional responsibility, a concept that is crucial for you to understand if you are to deal effectively when people accuse you of causing them to feel a certain way.

Cognitive Behavioural Therapy

You have probably have heard of Cognitive Behavioural Therapy (CBT). This is a therapeutic tradition that is made up of different approaches, most of which share one major principle: that our disturbed feelings are largely determined by the way we think. This is summed up by a phrase that is attributed to Epictetus, the Greek Stoic philosopher:

People are disturbed not by things, but by the views that they take of things.

Rational-Emotive Cognitive Behavioural Therapy

Within the CBT tradition there are about a dozen distinct approaches. This book is based on one of them, known as 'Rational Emotive Behavioural Therapy' (REBT), an approach to CBT that was originated by the noted American psychologist Dr Albert Ellis (1913–2007). REBT's basic position is a modification of Epictetus's dictum:

People are not disturbed by things. Rather, they disturb themselves by the rigid and extreme beliefs that they hold about things.

These rigid and extreme beliefs are known collectively as irrational beliefs because they are false, illogical and unconstructive. I refer to this approach as 'Rational-Emotive Cognitive Behavioural Therapy' (RECBT) to denote that, while it is firmly in the CBT tradition, its distinctiveness is REBT.

While RECBT argues that irrational beliefs are at the core of our disturbed emotions, it also notes that these beliefs influence the way in which we subsequently act and think and that such behaviour and thinking serve to perpetuate our disturbed emotions. I will discuss this in greater depth in Chapter 2.

Emotional responsibility vs 'You have upset me'

RECBT is based on the principle of emotional responsibility. As shown above, this means that when a person has disturbed feelings about a negative event (henceforth known as an adversity in this book), then these feelings are based largely on the rigid and extreme beliefs that the person holds about the adversity. So, while the adversity contributes to the person's disturbed feelings – after all, if the adversity had not occurred, he (in this case) would not have felt disturbed – what contribute much more to his disturbed feelings are his beliefs. Since the person holds these beliefs, he can be said to be responsible for holding them and therefore, by extension, for the disturbed feelings that stem from these beliefs. However, just because the person is responsible for his disturbed feelings, it does not follow that he should be depreciated or depreciate himself for making himself disturbed.

Let me now compare the principle of emotional responsibility with the views expressed by people who blame you for causing their disturbed feelings. In order for me to do this, I will first outline what in RECBT is known as the 'ABC' framework. In this framework, 'A' stands for adversity,[1] 'B' stands for beliefs and 'C' stands for the consequences of these beliefs. These consequences refer to the emotions that the person feels about the adversity, how he tends to act in the face of the adversity and how he subsequently thinks about the adversity once he has disturbed himself about it.

Let me use a specific example to make this comparison clear.

Mary's mother asked her to go shopping with her but Mary declined, saying that she had already promised to go for a coffee with a friend. Mary's mother became very hurt and blamed Mary for making her feel hurt.

Who is responsible for Mary's mother's feelings? 'B' largely determines 'C'

Here is the RECBT perspective on who is responsible for Mary's mother's feelings using the 'ABC' framework.

---

[1] See pp. 4–7 for a full discussion of what constitutes an adversity.

'A' = *My daughter has rejected me*
'B' = *My daughter must not reject me. It's terrible that she has.*
Poor me!
'C' = *Hurt.*

Conclusion

As we can see, while Mary's rejection of her mother (as her mother saw it) contributed to her mother's hurt feelings, her mother largely created these feelings with her own rigid and extreme beliefs. Therefore, Mary's mother is largely responsible for her feelings because she is largely responsible for the beliefs that she holds. In RECBT, we call the position '"B" largely determines "C"' the principle of emotional responsibility.

Who is responsible for Mary's mother's feelings? 'A causes C'

Here is Mary's mother's perspective on the same episode.

'A' = *My daughter has rejected me*
'C' = *Hurt.*

Conclusion

From Mary's mother's perspective, Mary has rejected her by not agreeing to go shopping with her in favour of having coffee with her friend. Her view is that this rejection, as she sees it, has caused her hurt and that Mary, therefore, is responsible for her hurt feelings.

If the position '"B" largely determines "C"' is called the principle of emotional responsibility, we could say that the position '"A" causes "C"' should be called the principle of emotional irresponsibility, since the person who is experiencing the feelings takes no responsibility for their creation. The principle of emotional irresponsibility is present when the other person blames you for causing his or her feelings.

Understanding the 'A' in the 'ABC' framework

As I have already discussed, in RECBT we use an 'ABC' framework to explain the principle of emotional responsibility. This model is simple but it is not simplistic, and where misunderstandings of the model occur these stem from confusion about what 'A' is. Originally, in RECBT, 'A' stood for 'activating event', which quite literally meant an event triggering a person's beliefs that explained the way she (in this case) felt, acted and subsequently thought. The problem with the concept of 'activating event' centred on the question 'What is an "event"?' Most people thought that an event reflected what actually happened. However, this is not quite the case.

Fact vs inference

In order to understand 'A', you need to distinguish between a fact and an inference. A fact, with respect to the concept of an 'event', is something that has happened and can be proved to have happened. While it is sometimes quite difficult to say that something has happened, this is what a fact is. An inference, on the other hand, is an interpretation of what has happened, which may be true or false. Its defining feature, however, is that it goes beyond the information that is at hand and needs to be tested out against the available data. Let me use the example of what happened between Mary and her mother to illustrate what I have said so far.

Mary and her mother: fact

Here is what actually happened between Mary and her mother. In other words, these are the facts:

- Mary's mother asked her to go shopping with her.
- Mary said 'no' and explained that she had already arranged to have coffee with a friend.

Mary and her mother: inference

We have already seen that Mary's mother was not reacting to the facts as outlined above. She was reacting to the inference that she made about the facts. In this case, we have the following from the perspective of Mary's mother:

- I asked Mary to come shopping with me.
- She said 'no' to my invitation to go shopping in favour of having coffee with her friend.

• This proves that Mary has rejected me.

As you can clearly see from this, the inference of rejection that Mary's mother drew from the facts (which appears in the third point above) goes beyond what actually happened.

Arguing about inferences: an exercise in futility

Initially, Mary responded to her mother by denying that she had rejected her. From her perspective, she had made a prior agreement to meet her friend and she was honouring that agreement. Her mother responded by saying that Mary cared more for her friend than she did about her, and the argument continued along these lines. What Mary was trying to do was to convince her mother of the facts, while her mother was reacting to her inference that Mary had rejected her. Because Mary's mother felt hurt about being rejected, this meant that she was not in a good frame of mind to discuss the facts of the matter with Mary. It was because Mary's mother felt hurt that she accused Mary of hurting her feelings by rejecting her.

This episode shows the following:

• People tend to experience disturbed emotions about inferences rather than about facts. Such an inference constitutes an adversity for the person making it.
• When people are disturbed about the inferences that they make, they are not in a sufficiently objective frame of mind to discuss the facts. Please bear this important point in mind, particularly when reading Chapter 5, which focuses on how to respond constructively when someone blames you for upsetting him or her.

Adversities at 'A' are often inferences, but are experienced as facts

The important point that you need to remember, then, is that the adversities that people react to in their lives are often inferences rather than facts. In the next chapter, I will discuss the emotions others experience that they are likely to blame you for causing. You will see there that different emotions are related to different adversities. While, as I have said, these adversities are inferences – meaning that they go beyond the information at hand and may be right or wrong – they are often experienced as facts by the person making them, particularly when that person has disturbed feelings about the adversity. Thus, if you remember, Mary's mother felt hurt (disturbed emotion) about being rejected by Mary (adversity) and considered that Mary's rejection of her was a fact rather than an inference. Furthermore, her hurt feelings meant that she was not in an objective frame of mind to stand back and consider the facts of the situation. This is precisely what Mary tried to get her mother to do, and it failed, as many such attempts will fail when the other person is in a disturbed frame of mind.

Let's assume that 'A' is true

In my other books for Sheldon Press, I have stated that when a person uses the 'ABC' framework to understand and deal with her own disturbed emotions, it is important for that person to accept temporarily that the inference that she made at 'A' is true. I suggest this to help the person look for and identify the irrational beliefs at 'B' that underpin her disturbed emotion at 'C'. In this book, I will encourage you to accept the adversity at 'A' as real for the other person. This will help you to avoid the futile arguments which will often ensue when you try to persuade someone who is in a disturbed frame of mind that what he or she thinks is real is not real.

Having discussed the principle of emotional responsibility in this chapter, in the following chapter I will help you to understand other people's emotions. This information will help you to withstand the viewpoint of others when they blame you for causing their emotions.

2

Understanding the disturbed emotions of others

Introduction

Knowledge is power: thus, when you are blamed for causing some-one's disturbed feelings,[1] it is important for you to know why this is not the case and what factors are involved in determining the person's feelings. So in this chapter I will discuss the RECBT position on the factors that are responsible for the eight disturbed emotions that people experience that they are likely to blame you for causing. These disturbed emotions are anxiety, depression, guilt, shame, hurt, unhealthy anger, unhealthy jealousy and unhealthy envy.

The 'ABC' framework of emotional disturbance: an overview

In Chapter 1, I introduced you to the idea that, according to RECBT, people disturb themselves about life's adversities because they hold a set of irrational (rigid and extreme) beliefs about the adversities. In this chapter, I will elaborate on this point by presenting the 'ABC' framework that we use in RECBT to make sense of people's disturbed emotions in the face of a variety of adversities. We also use it to show how people can deal constructively with the same adversities, but I won't discuss this point here.[2] So let me outline the 'ABC' framework, which I will use throughout this chapter and, indeed, in the rest of this book.

---

[1] People may also blame you for their healthy negative emotions, and if this is the case the same principles in this book apply. However, I will only discuss here how to deal with being blamed for people's disturbed emotions.

[2] See my book *Eight Deadly Emotions: What they are and how to deal with them* (Sheldon Press, 2012) for how to deal constructively with disturbed emotions.

- 'A' = Adversity
- 'B' = Irrational beliefs
- 'C' = Emotional consequences
     = Behavioural consequences
     = Thinking consequences.

'A' = Adversity

People disturb themselves about adversities. These can be actual events where it is clear what has happened, but more often they are inferences that people draw about what has happened to them. These may be true or false but need to tested against the available information. If you recall from Chapter 1, Mary's mother invited her to go shopping, an invitation that Mary declined because she had already agreed to have coffee with a friend. Mary's mother felt hurt about the inference that she drew from this situation – that Mary had rejected her. In this episode, rejection was Mary's mother's adversity.

'B' = Irrational beliefs

In RECBT, we argue that people are not disturbed by adversities. Rather, they disturb themselves by the rigid and extreme beliefs that they hold about these adversities. However, they do have a choice here. If they hold a set of flexible and non-extreme beliefs about the same adversities, then they will still feel bad about their existence (actual or presumed), but these negative feelings will be healthy and will be associated with constructive ways of acting and realistic forms of thinking that will help them deal effectively with the adversities.

It is important for you to understand that when people are disturbed about something that you have done (or failed to do), they have a choice that is relevant to the theme of this book.

- They could blame you for causing their disturbed feelings.
- They could take responsibility for their disturbed feelings and, while acknowledging that you may have contributed to their feelings, they could recognize that they are largely disturbed about what you did (or failed to do). Therefore, they need to address and change the factors that account for their disturbance, which in RECBT we say are the rigid and extreme beliefs that they held about what you did (or failed to do).

If you understand that people have largely disturbed themselves about what you did (or failed to do) then, when they hold you responsible or blame you for causing their disturbed feelings, you will know that this is not the case. If you digest and internalize this point you will not get caught up in fruitless arguments with the other person on this issue. In Chapter 5, I will discuss how to respond effectively when the other person blames you for disturbing him or her.

So, to recap, an adversity at 'A' doesn't cause a person's disturbed emotions. Rather, those feelings are largely determined by the irrational beliefs that he (in this case) holds about the adversity. As I pointed out above, in RECBT we argue that there are two types of irrational beliefs: rigid beliefs and extreme beliefs that are derived from these rigid beliefs. I will now discuss these so that you can understand the other person's belief system when he is disturbing himself about what you did (or did not do) and is blaming you for causing these disturbed feelings.

Rigid beliefs

When a person holds a rigid belief he begins by asserting his desire (e.g. 'I want you to be nice to me . . .'). Then he transforms this desire into a rigidity ('. . . therefore you must be'). Typically, rigid demands are most often stated without the asserted desire (e.g. 'You must be nice to me').

As I mentioned above, extreme beliefs tend to be derived from rigid beliefs. There are three such extreme beliefs:

- *Awfulizing beliefs* Here the person believes that it is awful or terrible that the adversity occurred (e.g. 'You must be nice to me and it would be terrible if you weren't').
- *Discomfort intolerance beliefs* Here the person believes that he cannot bear the adversity (e.g. 'You must be nice to me and I would not be able to bear it if you weren't').
- *Depreciation beliefs* Here the person depreciates himself, another person or life conditions, depending upon who he holds responsible for the existence of the adversity (e.g. 'You must be nice to me and you are bad if you don't act this way').

'C' = Consequences of holding irrational beliefs at 'B'

When a person holds a set of irrational beliefs at 'B' in the 'ABC' framework, then he or she will experience three major sets of consequences:

- *Emotional consequence* Here the person experiences what we call in RECBT an unhealthy negative emotion.
- *Behavioural consequence* Here the person experiences an urge to act or actually acts in a way that is consistent with his or her underpinning irrational beliefs and the associated unhealthy negative emotion.
- *Thinking consequence* Here the person thinks in a way that is consistent with his or her underpinning irrational beliefs and the associated unhealthy negative emotion.

I will now use the 'ABC' framework to help you understand the eight disturbed emotions that people will hold you responsible for or blame you for causing.

'You frighten me': what determines anxiety

When a person is anxious he (in this case) makes an inference that he is facing some kind of threat. This threat may be to the person's self-esteem or to his sense of comfort. Then he brings to this inference a rigid demand, with in ego anxiety a self-depreciation belief and in non-ego anxiety an awfulizing belief or a discomfort intolerance belief.

Then, when he feels anxious he will tend to act and think in certain ways that are designed to keep him safe from the threat but in fact make matters worse for him.

- 'A' = Threat
- 'B' = Irrational beliefs
- 'C' (emotional) = Anxiety
    (behavioural) = Designed to keep one safe from threat
    (thinking) = Safety-seeking or threat-exaggerating.

When a person blames you for making him feel anxious, he experiences you as threatening him in a certain way. Thus you may be threatening his sense of self-esteem or his sense of comfort (broadly defined). Then, when you make him feel anxious, as he sees it, he will try to avoid you, withdraw from you or to try to neutralize what he finds threatening about you (e.g. by being very nice to you to stop you being nasty to him).

Maurice

Maurice was frightened of his work colleague, Barry, whom he saw as confident and debonair while seeing himself as unconfident and socially awkward. Maurice would avoid Barry whenever he could and was mortified when their boss put them together to make a joint presentation for the company's bid for a business account. The way Maurice saw it, Barry made him feel anxious because when he was in Barry's presence he was flooded with thoughts of inadequacy. It transpired that they did not win the account, and in the company debrief later Maurice told Barry – in front of his boss – that he could not work well with Barry because he frightened him.

'You make me so depressed': what determines depression

When a person is depressed, she (in this case) makes an inference that she has experienced a loss from her personal domain, failed in some way or has experienced some undeserved plight. These inferences may be related to the autonomous realm of the personal domain (where the person values freedom, autonomy and effectiveness) or to the sociotropic realm (where she values her connection with others). Once the person has made such an inference, she then brings to it a rigid demand and an extreme belief.

Then, when she feels depressed she will tend to withdraw from life and think that things are far worse than they actually are and that she is helpless to do anything about her plight.

- 'A' = Loss, failure, undeserved plight
- 'B' = Irrational beliefs
- 'C' (emotional) = Depression
     (behavioural) = Withdrawal into oneself
     (thinking) = Hopelessness, helplessness.

When a person blames you for making her feel depressed, she thinks, for example, that you have rejected her or that being around you has led her to think that she has failed in some way and that you have made her feel that she is worthless. Then, when she is depressed she will withdraw from you or complain about you or to you.

Jenny

Jenny had been dating Will for over two years and the relationship was going well. Then, at a works party, Will spent the evening with Dianne, a work colleague. He was so besotted with Dianne that he abruptly ended his relationship with Jenny, who became depressed. Jenny's depression was based on the idea that Will had rejected her, that he absolutely should not have rejected her in favour of another woman and that she was worthless as a result. When Will came to pick up some possessions from Jenny's flat, she told him that he had made her depressed.

'You have guilt-tripped me': what determines guilt

When a person feels guilt she (in this case) makes an inference that she has done something wrong, has failed to do the right thing or has hurt someone's feelings. Then she brings to this inference a rigid demand and a self-depreciation belief.

Thus, when she feels guilt she will tend to act and think in certain ways which are designed to punish herself and which result in her exaggerating her sense of wrongdoing and responsibility:

- 'A' = Did the wrong thing; failed to do the right thing; hurt someone's feelings

- 'B' = Irrational beliefs
- 'C' (emotional) = Guilt
      (behavioural) = Designed to punish oneself
      (thinking) = Assumes a greater sense of responsibility than is warranted.

When a person blames you for making her feel guilty, what she is really saying is that you have succeeded in persuading her that she is bad for doing the wrong thing, failing to do the wrong thing or hurting someone's feelings.

Samantha
Samantha was visiting her sister Charlotte and looked surprised when Charlotte shouted at her young son. Charlotte caught Samantha's facial expression, which she inferred was disapproving, and accused Samantha of making her feel guilty.

'You have made me so ashamed to be a member of this family': what determines shame

When a person feels shame, he (in this case) makes an inference that he (or someone representing a group with whom he closely identifies) has fallen very short of his ideal. Then, he brings to this inference a rigid demand and a self-depreciation belief.

When the person feels ashamed, he will tend to think that others are viewing him with scorn and he then acts in ways designed to remove him from the scornful gaze of others.

- 'A' = Fallen very short of one's ideal (self or reference group member)
- 'B' = Irrational beliefs
- 'C' (emotional) = Shame
      (behavioural) = Designed to remove oneself from the scornful gaze of others
      (thinking) = Others will view self as defective, disgusting or diminished.

When a person blames you for making him feel ashamed, then he claims that you have acted in a way that falls very short of the ideal proposed by the reference group you have in common and that your actions have made him feel ashamed.

Fahid
Fahid was a Muslim who met and dated a Hindu girl. He knew how his family would respond so he tried to keep his relationship with her secret. However, his sister found out and accused Fahid of bringing shame on their family.

'You have really hurt my feelings': what determines hurt

When a person feels hurt, she (in this case) makes an inference that someone close to her has treated her badly and that she has done nothing to deserve such treatment, or that someone thinks less of his or her relationship with her than she does. Then, she brings to this inference a rigid demand and either a self-depreciation belief (in 'less me' hurt) or a discomfort intolerance belief (in 'poor me' hurt).

When the person feels hurt, she will tend to think and act in ways that shut down communication with you, but in such a way that you know that she is upset with you.

- 'A' = The person feels that someone close has treated her unfairly or devalued his or her relationship with her
- 'B' = Irrational beliefs
- 'C' (emotional) = Hurt
    (behavioural) = Sulking
    (thinking) = Thinking of past hurts and unfairness.

When a person blames you for her hurt feelings she claims that you have treated her unfairly or that you think less of your relationship with her than she does, and that your actions have made her feel hurt.

Brenda
Brenda heard on the grapevine that Muriel, her best friend, had been invited to a party and did not tell her that she was going. Brenda felt hurt about Muriel's omission and after sulking for two weeks told Muriel that she had hurt her (i.e. Brenda's) feelings by not telling her.

'You make me so angry when you won't listen to me': what determines unhealthy anger

When a person feels unhealthy anger, he (in this case) makes an inference that someone has broken a personal rule, frustrated him in some way or has disrespected him. Then, he brings to this inference a rigid demand and an other-depreciation belief.

When the person feels unhealthy anger, he will tend to think and act in ways that blame the other person and are aggressive to him or her.

- 'A' = The person feels that someone has broken his personal rule, frustrated him or disrespected him
- 'B' = Irrational beliefs
- 'C' (emotional) = Unhealthy anger
    (behavioural) = Designed to attack the other
    (thinking) = Planning to exact revenge.

When a person blames you for making him feel unhealthily angry, then he claims that you have disrespected him, frustrated him or broken his personal rule and that your actions have made him feel unhealthily angry.

Harry
Harry was waiting in a long queue for advance tickets when someone surreptitiously joined the queue in front of him. Harry responded with fury and shouted at the person with such venom that the station police were called. Explaining to them what had happened, Harry turned to the person who had jumped the queue and said, 'You made me angry by acting selfishly and barging ahead of me in the queue.'

'You made me mad with jealousy when you flirted with that man at the party': what determines unhealthy jealousy

When a person feels unhealthily jealous, he (in this case) makes an inference that someone poses a threat to his relationship and/or that he is uncertain about his partner's feelings, thoughts, behaviour or whereabouts. Then, he brings to these inferences a rigid demand and either a self-depreciation belief (related to his ability to keep his partner) or a discomfort intolerance belief (related to his state of uncertainty).

When the person feels unhealthy jealousy, he will tend to think in ways that exaggerate the nature of the threat that he perceives to his relationship and will act in ways that are designed to keep himself safe from that threat, but that are based on not trusting his partner.

- 'A' = The person feels that someone poses a threat to his relationship; he experiences uncertainty about the thoughts, feelings, behaviour and whereabouts of his partner
- 'B' = Irrational beliefs
- 'C' (emotional) = Unhealthy jealousy
  (behavioural) = Seeking certainty that one's relationship is not under threat
  (thinking) = Exaggerating the nature of that threat.

When a person blames you for his unhealthy jealousy he claims that you have acted in a way that poses a threat to your relationship with him and that your actions have caused his jealousy.

Melvin
Melvin took his girlfriend, Noreen, to his works party. Noreen enjoyed the party and particularly enjoyed talking to Malcolm, Melvin's work colleague, who she found witty but unattractive physically. Melvin became very jealous while watching Noreen laughing at Malcolm's witticisms. Melvin did not contact Noreen for over two weeks, refusing to return her increasingly frantic phone calls. When Melvin

did finally talk to Noreen he told her that the reason he did not want to talk to her was that she had made him jealous at the party.

'You like to make me really envious of you, don't you?': what determines unhealthy envy

When a person feels unhealthily envious, she (in this case) makes an inference that someone has something that she prizes, but does not have. Then, she brings to this inference a rigid demand and either a self-depreciation belief (in unhealthy ego envy) or an awfulizing belief/discomfort intolerance belief (in unhealthy non-ego envy).

When the person feels unhealthy envy, she will tend to think in ways that are designed to equalize things (either planning get the desired object or thinking how to spoil things for the other person) and will act in ways that are also designed to make things equal.

- 'A' = The person feels that someone has something that she prizes, but does not have
- 'B' = Irrational beliefs
- 'C' (emotional) = Unhealthy envy
    (behavioural) = Striving to get the prized object, depriving the person of the object or spoiling it for him or her
    (thinking) = Thinking how to get the prized object, how to deprive the other of the object or how to spoil it for him or her.

When a person blames you for her unhealthy envy, she claims that you have deliberately flaunted the objects you have that she does not have and that you know she covets in order to make her feel envious.

Laura

Laura was a wealthy woman who had worked hard for her money. She liked to look smart and would buy the latest fashionable shoes and handbags. Laura had two close friends, Jean and Fiona, and while Fiona was unconcerned with the latest fashions, Jean felt unhealthily envious of Laura for being able to buy what she prized but could not afford. When a minor tiff escalated into a major row, one of the triggers was Jean accusing Laura of enjoying making her feel envious of her by 'parading around' in the newest 'must-haves'.

In the next chapter, I will help you to understand why others blame you for their disturbed feelings. This information will be of help to you in dealing effectively with being accused of upsetting others.

3

Why others blame you for upsetting them

Introduction

So far in this book, I have explained the principle of emotional responsibility and outlined the factors in play when people disturb themselves about what you have done or failed to do and when they subsequently blame you for upsetting them. In this chapter, I will discuss the most common reasons why people blame you for upsetting them. These are as follows:

- People blame you for upsetting them because they do not know about the principle of emotional responsibility.
- People blame you for upsetting them because they have objections to the principle of emotional responsibility.
- People blame you for upsetting them to avoid blaming themselves.
- People blame you upsetting them because they do not know how to change their disturbed feelings.
- People blame you for upsetting them to avoid working to change their disturbed feelings.
- People blame you for upsetting them so that they can feel sorry for themselves.

People do not know about the principle of emotional responsibility

One of the reasons why you may be blamed for upsetting someone is that he or she does not know about the principle of emotional responsibility that I introduced and discussed in Chapter 1. If you recall, this principle states that people disturb themselves about your behaviour (for example) because they hold rigid and extreme beliefs about it. This does not mean that your behaviour does not contribute to their disturbed feelings, because it does – after all, if you had not acted in the way you did, they would not have disturbed themselves. However, a contribution is not a cause, and even though you acted in the way you did, the person still had a choice of whether to disturb him or herself about your behaviour by holding a set of irrational (rigid and extreme) beliefs about what you did, or not to disturb him or herself[1] by holding a set of rational (flexible and non-extreme beliefs) about your behaviour.

Most people do not know about the principle of emotional responsibility. If they learn about it and then stop blaming you for upsetting them, then it is clear that the main reason why they blamed you for causing their disturbed feelings was that they lacked this understanding. Once such people learn about the principle of emotional responsibility, they apply it and seek to discover the internal factors (i.e. irrational beliefs) that are largely responsible for their disturbed feelings. If they do this, they will not blame you for upsetting them.

However, even if people learn about the principle of emotional responsibility there may be other reasons why they still blame you for upsetting them, which I will now discuss.

People blame you for upsetting them because they have objections to the principle of emotional responsibility

Once a person learns about the principle of emotional responsibility, she (in this case) may well understand the concept but have doubts, reservations or objections to it. In this case, the person will not apply this principle and will continue to blame you for causing her disturbed feelings.

While there are a number of such doubts, let me discuss the two most commonly expressed ones and show why they are, in fact, misconceptions.

---

[1] By non-disturbed here, I mean that although the person will still have a negative response, this will be a non-disturbed one.

Objection 1: The principle of emotional responsibility lets you off the hook

Perhaps the most commonly expressed objection to the principle of emotional responsibility centres on the idea that when I disturb myself about your bad behaviour, if I take responsibility for upsetting myself then I am letting you off the hook. If a person holds this objection then she will see that she has only two choices: take emotional responsibility and let you off the hook, or blame you and refuse to take emotional responsibility herself.

Actually, there is a third option. I can take responsibility for my feelings and still hold you to account for your behaviour. Remember this if you encounter this objection to the principle of emotional responsibility if and when you teach it to someone who has blamed you for upsetting him or her.

Objection 2: Minor adversities may not cause my disturbed feelings, but major ones do

A person may accept that she (in this case) is responsible for upsetting herself if the adversity is minor, but may not do so if the adversity is major. This is a misconception, for the following reason: if it is the case that a person disturbs herself by holding a set of irrational beliefs about a minor adversity, it is also the case that she disturbs herself by holding a set of irrational beliefs about a major adversity. In both cases, if the person holds a set of rational beliefs about the adversity she will experience a healthy (non-disturbed) negative emotion. Consequently, it makes little sense to say that I disturb myself about minor adversities, but that major adversities disturb me.

My friend and colleague Paul Hauck, author of several self-help books for Sheldon Press, has made a very good point on this issue. If we take the 'ABC' framework and say that a disturbed emotion at 'C' is equal to a value of 100 per cent, then an adversity at 'A' can only account for up to 49 per cent of this disturbed emotion, the rest being determined by the person's irrational beliefs at 'B'. Thus, the more negative the adversity, the higher the percentage up to a ceiling of 49 per cent is the contribution of this event to the disturbed emotion. So, even when an adversity is very major, the person still has responsibility for disturbing him or herself to the value of 51 per cent upwards.

People blame you for upsetting them to avoid condemning themselves for their feelings

Imagine that you are faced with a choice of blaming someone else for upsetting you or condemning yourself for upsetting yourself, what would you do? You would probably blame the other person for upsetting you. This is what many people do when they think they are faced with such a stark choice. However, there is a third option: to take responsibility for largely creating your feelings but without blaming yourself. If some people who blamed you for upsetting them realized that they could accept themselves rather than condemning themselves for taking emotional responsibility, they might well stop blaming you.

Since this group of people are motivated to avoid self-condemnation, you need to be quite careful when discussing with them the episode in which they felt upset and subsequently blamed you for upsetting them. While you will not wish to take responsibility for upsetting them, you also need to avoid saying anything critical about their response which they would find a threat to their self-esteem. If you did say something critical about their response they would blame you for upsetting them about that as well! To avoid being critical, you will need to be in a rational frame of mind and therefore you will first need to un-disturb yourself about being blamed for upsetting the other person before discussing with him or her the episode in question (see Chapter 5).

People blame you for upsetting them because they do not know how to change their feelings

Let's assume that someone understands and agrees with the principle of emotional responsibility and accepts himself (in this case) for largely creating his own upset. Why might that person continue to blame you for upsetting him? One reason lies in the fact that such upset (or what we call unhealthy negative emotions in RECBT) is painful to experience. Humans are strongly motivated to try to get rid of pain (physical and emotional) as quickly as possible, unless there is a good reason for them not to do so. So even if a person accepts without self-condemnation the principle of emotional responsibility, he may not know what to do to deal effectively with his disturbed emotions. He is stuck with these feelings, so to speak. As a result, blaming you for upsetting him is a fairly quick way of getting rid of his upset. Of course, by blaming you he still feels upset, but this upset may be less painful than the original upset because the person may feel justified in blaming you.

If you are responding to this group of people you again need first to un-disturb yourself about being blamed for upsetting them, and then you need to offer them some information that they can use to deal with their original upset. My book for Sheldon Press (2012) entitled *Eight Deadly Emotions: What they are and how to deal with them* may just be what the doctor ordered! However, just because they could do with understanding their disturbed emotions and how to deal with them, it does not follow that they have to look at such information or that they have to use it if they do look at it. They are perfectly entitled not to gain and use such insight, and if they don't they may well continue to blame you for upsetting them. However, you will now understand why they do it.

People blame you for upsetting them to avoid working to change their feelings

I will now assume that someone understands the principle of emotional responsibility and accepts it without self-condemnation. I will further assume that the person knows how to deal with his (in this case) disturbed emotions. Why should the person continue to blame you for upsetting him, rather than applying the principles of emotional responsibility and the knowledge that he now has concerning how to deal effectively with his disturbed emotions?

Here is my perspective on this state of affairs. Dealing with emotional problems is hard work and some people bring their discomfort intolerance beliefs and related demands to this hard work. The result of this is that it is easier for them to blame you for upsetting them than it is for them to do the hard work of focusing on and dealing with their disturbed emotions related to you. Such people do not realize that they will spare themselves much upset if they do deal with their disturbed emotions, but their need to avoid hard work stops them from seeing the bigger picture. So if the person who blames you for upsetting him does so because it is the easier option, understanding his motivation may help you as you strive to do the hard work of un-disturbing yourself about his blame.

People blame you for causing their disturbed feelings so that they can feel sorry for themselves

For some people, feeling sorry for oneself is a familiar and satisfying emotional state, particularly when other people offer them sympathy for their undeserved plight. The need for sympathy can be quite powerful, and if such sympathy is given it leads the person to be further entrenched in a 'poor me' position. So, rather than dealing with their disturbed emotions related to you and achieving a measure of emotional health, such people blame you for upsetting them. In effect, they are playing the role of victim. In order to play this role fully, the person needs to deny that he or she has done anything to justify being treated badly by you.

Putting all this together, if such a person could fully articulate her attitude it would sound something like this: 'This other person (namely you!) has acted badly towards me and upset me and I did nothing to deserve this. This is so unfair and it really shouldn't have happened to me. Poor me!'

If you try and persuade the person that this is not the case and that, in fact, she has emotional responsibility and is disturbing herself about your behaviour, do not be surprised if this goes down like the proverbial lead balloon! Indeed, taking this tack will only give the person additional ammunition to play the 'poor me' victim card. Self-pity is fairly easy to spot and it is helpful to understand it when such a person blames you for upsetting her.

In the next chapter, I will consider the different ways in which people disturb themselves about being blamed for upsetting others. Understanding this is crucial if you are to implement the step-by-step guide that I will present in Chapter 5.

4

Why you respond unhealthily to being blamed for upsetting others

Introduction

In this chapter, I will discuss some of the major ways in which you may disturb yourself about being for blamed for upsetting people. In the following chapter, I will discuss what you need to do to address these disturbed responses effectively, so that you can, if need be, respond healthily to the other person when she blames you for upsetting her.

Understanding the nature of 'A'

Before I consider the different ways that people disturb themselves about being held responsible or blamed for causing the disturbed emotions of others, I want to revisit RECBT's 'ABC' framework and make sure that you understand the nature of 'A' in that framework. While I have discussed 'A' fully in Chapters 1 and 2, it is an elusive concept and one that bears further explanation.

In what follows, I will assume that you have been blamed for upsetting someone. When you disturb yourself about this, then your disturbed emotion points to what you find particularly disturbing about being thus blamed. What you find particularly disturbing is the 'A' in the 'ABC' framework. In Chapter 2, I examined each of the eight disturbed emotions that others blame you for causing and I suggest that you review this material if you need to. In this chapter, I will consider the main disturbed emotions that people have when they are blamed for upsetting others. These are: anxiety, depression, guilt, shame, hurt and unhealthy anger. Before I consider each in turn, I will summarize in Table 4.1 the main 'A's that are associated with these disturbed emotional responses to being blamed for causing others' emotional upset.

Table 4.1 What people tend to disturb themselves about when they are held responsible for or blamed for upsetting someone

When someone holds you responsible for or blames you for causing his or her disturbed emotion,

You experience at 'C'	You are most disturbed at 'A' that . . .
Anxiety	• There exists a threat to your self-esteem or sense of comfort.
Depression	• You have lost the affection of someone important to you. • You have failed. • An undeserved plight has befallen you.
Guilt	• You have done something wrong. • You have failed to do the right thing. • You have hurt someone's feelings.
Shame	• You have fallen far short of your ideal. • You have let down your reference group.
Hurt	• You have been unfairly treated by the other person.
Unhealthy anger at others	• The other person has broken one of your personal rules. • The other person has threatened your self-esteem.
Unhealthy self-anger	• You have broken one of your own personal rules.

Anxiety about being held responsible for or blamed for disturbing others

You make yourself anxious about someone blaming you for upsetting her (in this case) when you find being blamed a threat to you in some way. As I discussed in Chapter 2, anxiety may be an unhealthy response to a threat to your self-esteem or to your sense of comfort (broadly defined). Then, when you feel anxious you will try to avoid the person, you will withdraw from her or you will to try to neutralize what you find threatening about her (e.g. by agreeing that you are responsible for upsetting her).

As you will recall, according to RECBT you experience anxiety because you hold a set of irrational beliefs about the threat that you face. Here are two case examples of people who made themselves anxious about threats related to the prospect of being blamed for upsetting someone.

Betty – a case of ego anxiety

Betty regarded herself as a dutiful wife but considered that her mother-in-law never gave her credit for this and, indeed, often felt upset with Betty's treatment of her son and blamed Betty for upsetting her. Whenever Betty visited her in-laws, she felt anxious about being thus blamed. Here is the 'ABC' analysis of Betty's anxiety, which was ego in nature.

- 'A' = My mother-in-law will blame me for upsetting her.
- 'B' = My mother-in-law must not blame me for upsetting her, and if she does it proves that I am a worthless person.
- 'C' (emotional) = Anxiety.
  (behavioural) = Drinking to tranquillize anxiety.
  (thinking) = If she holds me responsible for upsetting her, she will hate me for ever.

John – a case of non-ego anxiety

John was anxious about being blamed by his aunt for making her feel ashamed of his behaviour, because of the conflict that would ensue between them. Here is an 'ABC' analysis of John's anxiety, which was non-ego in nature.

- 'A' = If my aunt blames me for making her feel ashamed, conflict will ensue.
- 'B' = I must not have conflict with my aunt and I could not bear it if it happened.
- 'C' (emotional) = Anxiety.
  (behavioural) = Avoiding going to see my aunt.
  (thinking) = If I have conflict with my aunt she will become very ill.

Depression about being blamed for upsetting others

You make yourself depressed when a person blames you for upsetting her for one of several reasons:

- You view her accusation as evidence that you have lost her affection.
- You consider that you have failed in some way by upsetting the person.
- You regard the accusation as representing an undeserved plight.

Then when you are depressed you will withdraw from that person while complaining about her.

As you will now know, according to RECBT you experience depression because you hold a set of irrational beliefs about loss, failure or undeserved plight. Here are three case examples of people who made themselves depressed about issues that were related to their being blamed for upsetting the disturbed feelings of others.

> *Melanie – a case of depression about losing the affection of someone*
> Melanie became depressed when her sister blamed Melanie for making her feel guilty. Melanie inferred that this meant that she had lost her sister's affection and made herself depressed about this loss. Here is an 'ABC' analysis of Melanie's depression.
>
> - 'A' = My sister blames me for making her feel guilty and this means that I have lost her affection.
> - 'B' = I must not lose my sister's affection and I am unlovable because I have done so.
> - 'C' (emotional) = Depression.
>   (behavioural) = Withdrawing into myself.
>   (thinking) = My entire family will reject me once they know what has happened.

Roger – a case of depression about failure

Roger became depressed when his daughter blamed him for making her feel ashamed of her body. Roger inferred that this meant that he had failed as a father and made himself depressed about this failure. Here is an 'ABC' analysis of Roger's depression.

- 'A' = My daughter blaming me for making her feel ashamed of her body means that I have failed as a father.
- 'B' = I must not fail as a father and I am a failure as a person if I do.
- 'C' (emotional) = Depression.
    (behavioural) = Drinking to get rid of my depressed feelings.
    (thinking) = My relationship with my daughter is ruined for ever.

Stella – a case of depression about an undeserved plight

Stella became depressed when one of her students blamed her for making him feel inadequate and made a formal complaint, which her college decided to investigate. Stella thought this was an undeserved plight and made herself depressed about it. Here is an 'ABC' analysis of Stella's depression.

- 'A' = I don't deserve to be in the unfair situation of being investigated by college for making one of my students feel inadequate.
- 'B' = I must not be in this undeserved plight and it's terrible that I am. Poor me!
- 'C' (emotional) = Depression.
    (behavioural) = Complaining about the situation to everyone.
    (thinking) = Ruminating about the unfairness of being in this undeserved plight.

Guilt about being blamed for upsetting others

When a person blames you for upsetting her and you feel guilty about this, you do so about one of the following themes:

- You think that you have done the wrong thing.
- You think that you have failed to do the right thing.
- You think that you have upset the person's feelings.

When you experience guilt under these circumstances, you will either avoid the person who has held you responsible for upsetting her or you will beg her to forgive you.

You will have grasped the point that, according to RECBT, you experience guilt because you hold a set of irrational beliefs about doing the wrong thing, not doing the right thing or hurting someone's feelings.

Here are three case examples of people who made themselves feel guilt about issues related to their being held responsible or blamed for causing the disturbed feelings of others.

Susan – a case of guilt about doing the wrong thing

Susan felt guilt when her mother blamed her for making her feel lonely. Susan inferred that this meant she had done the wrong thing by neglecting her mother and made herself guilty about this. Here is an 'ABC' analysis of Susan's guilt.

- 'A' = I have done the wrong thing by neglecting my mother.
- 'B' = I absolutely should not have done the wrong thing by neglecting my mother and I am a bad person for doing so.
- 'C' (emotional) = Guilt.
    (behavioural) = Begging her to forgive me.
    (thinking) = My mother will never forgive me.

Ben – a case of guilt about not doing the right thing

Ben was invited to a party with a group of friends. Unbeknown to him, one of his friends, Martin, was not invited, and Ben only discovered this when Martin did not show up at the party. When Martin found out that Ben and the others had gone to the party to which he was not invited, he felt hurt and blamed his friends for causing his hurt feelings. Ben responded to Martin's accusation with guilt. What Ben felt guilty about was that he did not do what he saw as the right thing, which was to tell Martin about the invitation when he received it. Here is an 'ABC' analysis of Ben's guilt.

- 'A' = I did not do the right thing and tell Martin that I was invited to the party.
- 'B' = I absolutely should have done the right thing and told Martin about the party invitation and I am bad for not doing so.
- 'C' (Emotional) = Guilt.
     (Behavioural) = Avoiding Martin.
     (Thinking) = I have lost Martin's friendship for ever.

Loretta – a case of guilt about hurting someone's feelings

Loretta forgot to send her grandmother a birthday card. She heard from her mother that her gran was very upset about this and held Loretta responsible for causing her hurt feelings. Loretta responded to this with guilt for hurting her gran's feelings. Here is an 'ABC' analysis of Loretta's guilt.

- 'A' = I hurt my gran's feelings by forgetting to send her a birthday card.
- 'B' = I absolutely should not have hurt her feelings and I am bad for doing so.
- 'C' (emotional) = Guilt.
     (behavioural) = Going over the top and sending my gran a very big bunch of flowers which I can't afford.
     (thinking) = I thought of all the other people in my life whose feelings I've hurt.

Shame about being blamed for upsetting others

When a person holds you responsible for or blames you for upsetting her and you feel ashamed, you do so about one of the following themes:

- You accept the proposition that you are responsible for upsetting her feelings and you infer that in doing so you have fallen far short of your ideal.

- You accept the proposition that you are responsible for upsetting her feelings and you infer that in doing so you have let down your reference group.

When you experience shame under these circumstances, you will avoid either (1) the person who has blamed you for upsetting her or (2) the relevant reference group.

Don't forget that you experience shame because you hold a set of irrational beliefs about falling short of your ideal or letting down your reference group.

Here are two case examples of people who made themselves feel ashamed about issues related to their being blamed for upsetting others.

Brian – a case of shame about falling short of one's ideal

Brian felt ashamed when his girlfriend's father blamed Brian for making him angry on discovering that, contrary to their agreement, Brian had kept his daughter out very late. Brian felt very ashamed about his actions, which he saw as him falling very short of what he expected of himself. Here is an 'ABC' analysis of Brian's shame.

- 'A' = I have fallen very short of my ideal by failing to keep my agreement with my girlfriend's father.
- 'B' = I absolutely should have kept my agreement and I am less of a person for not doing so.
- 'C' (emotional) = Ashamed.
  (behavioural) = Staying away from my girlfriend and her father.
  (thinking) = I have ruined my relationship with my girlfriend.

Mandira – a case of shame about letting down one's reference group

Mandira came from a family who all got first-class degrees from Cambridge University. However, despite working very hard Mandira was awarded an upper second rather than a first and her family were very upset about what they regarded as her failure. They blamed Mandira for bringing shame to the family. Mandira responded to this by feeling ashamed about letting her family down. Here is an 'ABC' analysis of Mandira's shame.

- 'A' = I have let my family down by not getting a first.
- 'B' = I absolutely should not have let my family down and I am defective for doing so.
- 'C' (emotional) = Ashamed.
  (behavioural) = Running away from home.
  (thinking) = I have dishonoured my family's good name for ever.

Hurt about being blamed for upsetting others

When a person blames you for upsetting her and you feel hurt about this, you do so because (1) you regard the accusation as very unfair and the person as having let you down by making it and (2) you hold a set of irrational beliefs about the unfair accusation. When you experience hurt under these circumstances, you will tend to cut off communication with the other and sulk until the person has come to you to put things right.

There are two types of hurt: ego hurt (where you conclude that you are less worthy) or non-ego hurt (where you feel sorry for yourself). Although in ego hurt you think that you do not deserve to be falsely accused, you also think that if you were a better person in some way, this would not have happened. In non-ego hurt, your focus is just on the unfairness. This will be demonstrated in the following case examples of people who made themselves feel hurt about an issue related to their being blamed for upsetting someone.

Jeremy – a case of ego hurt about being accused unfairly of upsetting someone

Jeremy was a GP and prided himself on his good relationships with his patients. However, one day one of his patients made a complaint about him to the practice manager, stating that Jeremy had made her feel small by dismissing her concerns about her cough. Jeremy felt hurt about this because he thought that the accusation was unjustified. Here is an 'ABC' assessment of Jeremy's hurt.

- 'A' = My patient has made an unfair accusation about me.
- 'B' = She must not be unfair towards me, but I am less worthy for perhaps not doing enough for her.
- 'C' (emotional) = Hurt.
      (behavioural) = Being over-solicitous to all my patients for the rest of the week.
      (thinking) = If I was a better GP this would not have happened.

Lesley – a case of non-ego hurt about being unfairly accused of upsetting someone

Lesley had always done a lot for her next-door neighbour, who had a hip problem and could not walk. Lesley would shop for her and generally run errands for the woman. One day, Lesley agreed to pick up her neighbour from a physiotherapy appointment but was held up in traffic. When she finally arrived, she was told that her neighbour had ordered a taxi and had left.

When Lesley got home, she went next door to apologize and her neighbour was very upset with her, claiming that Lesley had made her angry by not picking her up. Lesley responded with hurt about this accusation, since she regarded it as unfair for two reasons: (1) her lateness in picking up her neighbour had been out of her control and (2) she had always helped out her neighbour whenever she could and considered that the latter had not taken any of this into account in her accusation. Here is the 'ABC' analysis of Lesley's hurt.

- 'A' = I don't deserve to be blamed for making my neighbour angry.
- 'B' = I must not be treated in such an unfair manner. I can't bear it. Poor me!
- 'C' (emotional) = Hurt.
      (behavioural) = Sulking.
      (thinking) = That is the very last time I help my neighbour. She can find someone else to help her.

Unhealthy anger about being blamed for upsetting others

When a person blames you for upsetting her and you are unhealthily angry about this, you are angry either towards her or towards yourself. As shown in Table 4.1 (see p. 28) you make one of the following inferences when you are unhealthily angry.

When your unhealthy anger is directed against others, you think that:

- the other person has broken one of your personal rules;
- the other person has threatened your self-esteem.

However, when your unhealthy anger is directed against yourself, then you think that:

- you have broken one of your own personal rules.

When you experience anger under these circumstances, your urge will be to attack the other person or yourself in some way. Here are three case examples of people who made themselves feel unhealthily angry about an issue related to their being blamed for upsetting someone.

Harry – a case of unhealthy anger about another who has broken one's personal rule

Harry believed strongly in the principle of emotional responsibility, discussed in Chapter 1. When his sister held him responsible for making her feel hurt, he responded with unhealthy anger. Here is an 'ABC' analysis of Harry's unhealthy anger.

- 'A' = By holding me responsible for making her feel hurt, my sister is not taking responsibility for her own feelings.
- 'B' = My sister must take responsibility for her feelings and she is an idiot for not doing so.

- 'C' (emotional) = Unhealthy anger.

  (behavioural) = Wanting to shake her and make her see sense.

  (thinking) = I am going to get her to see the error of her irre-sponsible ways, if it's the last thing I do.

Debbie – a case of unhealthy anger about another threatening one's self-esteem

On a visit to her uncle and aunt, Debbie accidentally broke a valuable vase. Her aunt was particularly upset and held Debbie responsible both for breaking the vase and for upsetting her. Debbie responded with unhealthy anger and left in a rage. Here is an 'ABC' analysis of Debbie's unhealthy anger.

- 'A' = My aunt made me feel badly about myself by blaming me for upsetting her.
- 'B' = She absolutely should not have made me feel badly about myself and she is bad for doing so.
- 'C' (emotional) = Unhealthy anger.

  (behavioural) = Leaving in a rage.

  (thinking) = I am really clumsy and don't take care with other people's possessions, but my aunt could have taken more care with my feelings.

Lawrence – a case of unhealthy self-anger about breaking one's own personal rule

It was important for Lawrence to have very good relationships with his family and friends. He was popular, but found it difficult to say 'no' to people who wanted to see him. As a result, he some-times double-booked arrangements and had to let someone down at the last minute. When he did this to Gina, she was very upset and accused him of making her angry. Lawrence reacted to this by becoming unhealthily angry with himself. Here is an 'ABC' analysis of Lawrence's unhealthy self-anger.

- 'A' = I broke my personal rule of not upsetting my family and friends by upsetting Gina.

- 'B' = I absolutely should not have broken my personal rule by upsetting Gina and I'm an unworthy person for doing so.
- 'C' (emotional) = Unhealthy self-anger.
    (behavioural) = Pacing up and down and swearing at myself.
    (thinking) = Ruminating about the incident.

In the next chapter, I will outline a step-by-step guide to responding healthily to being blamed for upsetting someone.

5

How to respond healthily to being blamed for upsetting others

Introduction

In this chapter, I will help you to deal constructively with one or more of the emotional problems that you may have when you are blamed for upsetting others. In doing so, I will make use of the 'ABC' framework that I discussed in Chapter 2. I will also draw on the material that I discussed in Chapter 4.

Before I start, let me make an important point. If you are emotionally disturbed about being blamed for upsetting others, then you will not be able to think clearly about how best to respond to such situations, and thus your behaviour will be likely to be unconstructive. In RECBT, we make a distinction between emotional problems and practical problems. We argue that when you have an emotional problem about a practical problem, it is best to address the emotional problem before you tackle the practical problem. In most cases, we find that when people have emotional problems about practical problems then these emotional problems generally interfere with practical problem-solving. Trying to tackle a practical problem while you are emotionally disturbed about it is like trying to walk up a steep hill with a ball and chain around one of your ankles. It's possible, but it's much, much harder when you do it this way.

When someone blames you for upsetting him or her and you are not disturbed about it, this represents a practical problem. In such a case your main concern will be how best to respond to the other person. When you are additionally disturbed about such an accusation, your disturbance will interfere with your thinking about how best to respond and thus, as I have already said, it will increase the chances that your actual response to the other will be unconstructive. This is why we in RECBT strongly suggest that you address

41

your emotional problem about being blamed for upsetting another person before you engage in practical problem-solving designed to respond constructively to that person.

How to deal with your emotional problems about being blamed for upsetting others

If you are prone to disturbing yourself about being blamed for upsetting others then you tend to do this in a variety of different settings and in response to a variety of different people. What follow are a number of steps that you can take to deal with your emotional problems so that you become less prone to this. Throughout the rest of the chapter, I will illustrate my points with the case of John, whom we first met in Chapter 4 (see p. 29).

Step 1: Specify your emotional problems about being held responsible for or blamed for upsetting others

In Chapter 4, I suggested that people tend to have six disturbed emotional reactions when they are blamed for upsetting people. These are anxiety, depression, guilt, shame, hurt and unhealthy anger. I suggest that you write down which of these disturbed emotions you are prone to when you are blamed for upsetting people.

> John considered that he had two emotional problems related to being blamed for upsetting people. These were anxiety and guilt, which he wrote down.

Step 2: Select and deal with one emotional problem at a time

In RECBT, we advise you to select and deal with one emotional problem at a time. We suggest this because otherwise you will get confused and easily side-tracked if you try and deal with two or more problems at once. When you make your selection, you can choose either the one disturbed emotion to which you are most prone or the one which is, in your opinion, the easiest to deal with. The main point I want to stress is that you should deal with one problem at a time and only begin to work on a second emotional problem once you have effectively dealt with the first. In RECBT, the emotional problem that you select to tackle is known as a 'target problem'.

John selected 'anxiety' as the emotional problem that he wanted to focus on and this became his target problem.

Step 3: Identify reasons why your target problem is a problem for you and why you want to change

While in RECBT we regard anxiety, depression, guilt, shame, hurt and unhealthy anger as disturbed emotions, it is useful for you to spell out reasons why your selected disturbed emotion is a problem for you and why you want to change. I suggest that you keep a written list of these reasons and refer to it as needed as a reminder of why you are engaged in a self-help programme. I will discuss the healthy alternatives to the six listed disturbed emotions in Step 6.

John considered his anxiety about issues to do with being blamed for upsetting others a problem for him for a number of reasons. He made a written note of these.

- His anxiety was very painful to experience.
- His anxiety led him to avoid those who he thought would blame him for upsetting them. If he could not avoid them, he would be extra nice towards them so that they would not feel upset with him.
- He felt very nervy and jumpy in the presence of those he thought were the kind of people who would blame him for upsetting them.

Step 4: Take responsibility for your target emotional problem

As I pointed out in Chapter 1, in RECBT we argue that being blamed for upsetting someone does not make you disturbed; rather, you create these disturbed feelings by the rigid and extreme beliefs that you hold about such accusations. You may object that this involves you blaming yourself for creating your disturbed feelings, but this objection is based on a misconception. It assumes that taking responsibility for creating your emotional problem is synonymous with self-blame. In truth, as I discussed in Chapter 1, responsibility means that you take ownership for the irrational beliefs that underpin your emotional problem while accepting yourself for doing so. Blame, on the other hand, means that you regard yourself as worthless for creating your emotional problem.

Originally, John blamed other people for making him anxious in the same way as he thought those people blamed him for upsetting them, whether this was actually the case or only in his mind. Then John read the first chapter in this book and Step 1 in my best-selling book for Sheldon Press, *Ten Steps to Positive Living* (1994), and these readings helped him to see that by blaming others he was not taking responsibility for his own feelings of anxiety. By seeing clearly that he made himself anxious about being blamed for upsetting others because he held a set of irrational beliefs about issues to do with being blamed in this way, John took personal responsibility for creating his own anxiety.

Step 5: Identify the themes at 'A' about which you disturb yourself and assume temporarily that they are true

In Table 4.1 (see p. 28), I outlined the types of adversities at 'A' about which you disturb yourself when others blame you for upsetting them. I suggest you consult this table for help with identifying the theme (at 'A') of your emotional problem.

When someone blames you for upsetting him or her in some way and you are disturbed about this, then you make an inference that is related to the particular disturbed emotion that you experience (see Table 4.1). For example, when you are anxious you infer the presence of a threat, and when you are ashamed you think that you have fallen short of your ideal in some way. You will recall that the RECBT 'ABC' framework posits that disturbed reactions at 'C' are largely determined by irrational beliefs at 'B' about actual or inferred adversities at 'A'. This model, therefore, stresses the importance of identifying, questioning and changing your irrational beliefs to their rational alternatives at 'B'. To do this you need to assume temporarily that the particular inferences that you make at 'A' and the broader themes that these are based on are true in order to move to 'B'. At this point, if you correct any distortions in particular inferences or broader themes at 'A' then you may feel better but you will not get better, a process dependent in large part on holding rational beliefs at 'A'. Changing distorted inferences or themes at 'A' (particularly when you feel better by doing so) means that you will be less motivated to identify, question and change your underlying irrational beliefs.

You will have a later opportunity to question 'A' after you have developed and rehearsed rational beliefs at 'B'.

After keeping a diary of his anxiety related to situations where he thought he would be blamed for upsetting others, John realized that he was most anxious about the conflict that he feared would ensue if he was accused of being thus responsible.

Step 6: Identify the three components of your disturbed response and set goals with respect to each component

The next step is for you to list the three elements of your disturbed response in the face of the themes that you identified in Step 5 and to set goals for each element. When you provide the information that I ask you for in this section, I suggest that you consult Appendix 1.[1] This specifies:

- the six unhealthy negative emotions (i.e. disturbed emotions) detailed above;
- the healthy negative emotional alternatives to each of these six unhealthy negative emotions;
- the thinking and behavioural components associated with each unhealthy negative emotion and healthy alternative.

---

[1]   In addition to the six unhealthy negative emotions discussed in this chapter, Appendix 1 also contains information about unhealthy jealousy and unhealthy envy and their healthy alternatives, which I discussed in Chapter 2.

Identify the three components of your disturbed response

I use the term 'disturbed response' to describe the three main components that make up this response. The three components of your disturbed response are as follows:

- *Emotional component* The emotional component is your unhealthy negative emotion (i.e. anxiety, depression, guilt, shame, hurt or unhealthy anger).
- *Behavioural component* The behavioural component concerns overt behaviour or action tendencies associated with each disturbed emotion (see Appendix 1).
- *Thinking component* The thinking component concerns the thinking that is associated with your target unhealthy negative emotion (see Appendix 1). Such thinking may be in words or in mental pictures.

The components of John's anxiety were as follows:

- Emotional component = Anxiety.
- Behavioural components = Avoidance of the relevant person or being extra nice to him or her.
- Thinking component = Thinking highly negative things will occur if conflict happens.

Set goals with respect to each of the three components

You need to set goals so that you know what you are striving for when you deal effectively with your target unhealthy negative emotion. The three components of your goal are as follows:

- *Emotional goal* Your emotional goal reflects the fact that you will still be facing the same adversity theme at 'A'. Therefore the emotion will be negative, but healthy in that it helps you to deal effectively with the adversity. Here are the emotional goals with respect to each of the six unhealthy negative emotions that I detailed above. These are:

- concern rather than anxiety
- sadness rather than depression
- remorse rather than guilt
- disappointment rather than shame
- sorrow rather than hurt
- healthy anger rather than unhealthy anger.

It is important that you realize that the terms I have used to represent the healthy negative emotions are not definitive or meant to be prescriptive. By all means use different terms if they are more meaningful to you.

- *Behavioural goal* Your behavioural goal should reflect actions that are based on the healthy negative emotional alternative to your target disturbed emotion (see Appendix 1).
- *Thinking goal* As well as setting behavioural goals related to your emotional goal, it is also important that you set thinking goals associated with this healthy negative emotion (see Appendix 1). Again, please remember that such thinking may be in words or in mental pictures.

John's goals with respect to the components of his anxiety were as follows:

- Emotional goal = Concern.
- Behavioural goal = Facing the relevant person without being extra nice to him.
- Thinking goal = Thinking that negative, positive or neutral events could occur if conflict happens.

Step 7: Identify your general irrational beliefs and alternative general rational beliefs

A general irrational belief is an irrational belief that you hold across situations defined by the theme that you are disturbed about. It accounts for your disturbed negative emotions. Its rational alternative, which will also be general in nature, will account for your healthy response (emotional, behavioural and thinking) to the same theme.

Identify your general irrational beliefs

When you identify a general irrational belief, you take a common theme (e.g. hurting someone's feelings or being treated unfairly) and add to this a general rigid belief and the main extreme belief that is derived from the rigid belief. For problems that involve self-esteem, then your main extreme belief will be a self-depreciation belief (e.g. 'I must not hurt someone's feelings and if I do it will prove that I am worthless'). For problems that are not based on self-esteem, your main extreme belief may be either an awfulizing belief or a discomfort intolerance belief (e.g. 'I must not be treated unfairly and I can't bear it when I am') and less frequently it may be an other-depreciation belief or a life-depreciation belief.

Identify your alternative general rational beliefs

When you identify your alternative general rational belief, you take the same common theme (e.g. hurting someone's feelings or being treated unfairly) and add to this a general flexible belief and the main non-extreme belief that is derived from the flexible belief. If your general extreme belief is self-depreciation, then your general non-extreme belief will be a self-acceptance belief (e.g. 'I don't want to hurt someone's feelings, but I don't have to be immune from doing so. If I do, I am not worthless. I am fallible'). If your general extreme belief underpins problems that are not based on self-esteem, then your alternative general non-extreme beliefs will be a non-awfulizing belief, a discomfort tolerance belief (e.g. 'I don't like being treated unfairly, but that does not mean that I must not be. If I am it is difficult to bear, but I can bear it and it's worth it to me to do so') and less frequently an other-acceptance belief or a life-acceptance belief.

John's general irrational belief was: 'I must not have conflict with people who are important to me and I could not bear it if it happened.'

His alternative rational belief was: 'I would prefer not to have conflict with people who are important to me, but that does not mean that it must not happen. If it did, it would be hard for me to bear, but I could do so and it would be worth it to me to do so.'

Step 8: Question your general beliefs

While there are many ways of questioning your general irrational beliefs and general rational beliefs, in my view the most efficient way involves two steps:

- First, question together your general rigid belief and your alternative general flexible belief.
- Then, question together your general extreme belief and your general non-extreme belief.

Question your general rigid belief and its general flexible belief alternative

First take your general rigid belief and its general flexible belief alternative and write them down next to one another on a sheet of paper. Then ask yourself:

- Which is true and which is false?
- Which is sensible and logical and which does not make sense?
- Which has largely constructive results and which has largely unconstructive results?

Write down your answer to each of these questions on your piece of paper. I suggest that you consult Appendix 2 for help with the answers to these questions, which you need to adapt and apply to the beliefs you are questioning.

Question your general extreme belief and its general non-extreme belief alternative

Then, take your general extreme belief and the general non-extreme belief alternative and again write them down next to one another on a sheet of paper. Now ask yourself the same three questions that you used with your general rigid belief and general flexible alternative belief. Again write down your answer to each of these questions on your piece of paper. I suggest that you consult Appendix 3 (for help with questioning awfulizing beliefs and non-awfulizing beliefs), Appendix 4 (for help with questioning discomfort intolerance beliefs and discomfort tolerance beliefs) and Appendix 5 (for help with questioning depreciation beliefs and acceptance beliefs). Again, you need to adapt and apply these arguments to the beliefs you are questioning.

You should now be ready to commit to acting and thinking in ways consistent with your general rational belief.

John argued that, while he could prove that having conflict with people was undesirable, he could not prove that as a result it must not happen. He showed himself that while he could avoid conflict with others by accepting the blame for upsetting them, he really did not want to do that, and stated that it was worth it to him to withstand any ensuing conflict, arguing that he could do so in order to assert himself with those who blamed him in this way.

Step 9: Rehearse your rational beliefs while facing in your imagination situations reflecting your theme at 'A'

Hopefully you have made a commitment to act on your general rational beliefs (i.e. flexible belief and relevant non-extreme belief). Assuming that you have, your basic task is to face up to situations reflecting your theme at 'A' while both rehearsing your rational beliefs and thinking and acting in ways that are consistent with these developing rational beliefs.

Up to this point you have worked at a general level with respect to the theme you are most disturbed about in your target problem. However, when you come to apply your general rational beliefs in dealing with this theme, you need to bear in mind one important point. Since you make yourself disturbed about the theme at 'A' in specific situations (actual or imagined), you need to deal with these specific threats by rehearsing specific variants of your general rational beliefs.

While the best way to do this is in specific situations in which you infer the presence of the theme, you may derive benefit from using imagery first. If this is the case with you, you need to do the following:

- Imagine a specific situation in which you felt disturbed and focus on the theme.
- See yourself facing the situation in which the theme is deemed to be present, and picture yourself rehearsing a specific rational belief relevant to the situation. As you do this, try to make yourself experience the healthy alternative to your unhealthy negative emotion (e.g. try to make yourself feel concerned rather than anxious).
- Then see yourself take appropriate action. Make your picture realistic. Picture a faltering performance with room for improvement rather than a masterful one that cannot be improved on.
- Recognize that some of your post-belief thinking may be distorted, Respond to it without getting bogged down doing so. Accept the presence of any remaining distorted thoughts without engaging with them.

Repeat the above steps until you feel sufficiently ready to face your theme in actuality.

If you find facing the situation that embodies the theme too much for you in your mind's eye, use a principle that I call 'challenging, but not overwhelming'. This means that instead of imagining yourself facing the situation that you first selected, you choose to face a similar situation embodying the same theme that you would find 'challenging, but not overwhelming'. Then employ the same steps that I have outlined above. Work in this way with modified situations embodying the theme until you find your original situation 'challenging, but not overwhelming' and then use the steps again.

John imagined himself rehearsing a specific version of his rational belief about conflict while asserting himself with his aunt who was blaming him for upsetting her. Thus, he showed himself that he could tolerate having conflict with his aunt and it was worth it to him to do so, as it was important for him to show her that he was no longer going to be manipulated by her attempts to make him feel bad for upsetting her. In this way, he showed himself that he did not have to avoid conflict with his aunt.

Step 10: Face your theme in reality

Whether or not you have used imagery as a preparatory step, you need to take the following steps when you face your theme in reality.

- Choose a specific situation in which the theme is embodied and about which you would ordinarily feel disturbed.
- Make a plan of how you are going to deal with the situation.
- Rehearse a specific version of your general rational beliefs before entering the situation so that you can face your theme while in a rational frame of mind. In addition, it would be useful to develop a shorthand version of your specific rational belief to use while you are in the situation.
- Enter the situation and accept the fact that you are likely to be uncomfortable while doing so. React to any consequences from a rational frame of mind if you can.
- Recognize that, even though you have got yourself into a rational frame of mind, some of your thinking may be distorted and unrealistic and some may be realistic and balanced. Accept the presence of the former and do not engage with it. Engage with the latter without using it to reassure yourself.

John developed a shorthand version of his rational belief (i.e. 'I can tolerate having conflict with my aunt and it's worth it to me to do so') which he rehearsed before, during and after he asserted himself with his aunt in an actual situation where she blamed him for upsetting her. He still had some distorted thought, especially directly after he stood his ground with his aunt, but he let such thoughts be, recognizing that they were thinking remnants of his irrational belief which he was acting against.

Step 11: Capitalize on what you have learned

When you have faced a situation that reflected the theme at 'A' and dealt with it as best you could, it is important that you reflect on what you did and what you have learned. In particular, if you were able to face your theme, rehearse your specific rational beliefs and take constructive action, then ask yourself how you can capitalize on what you have achieved. If you experienced any problems, respond to the following questions:

- Did I face the theme, and if not, why not?
- Did I rehearse my rational beliefs before and during facing the theme, and if not, why not?
- Did I execute my plan to face the theme, and if not, why not?
- Did I engage with post-belief distorted thinking, and if so, why?

Reflect on your experience and put into practice what you have learned the next time you face the theme.

John reflected on applying what he had learned with his aunt and was pleased in principle with what he did. However, he realized that he had avoided looking at her while asserting himself with her. He resolved to look at the person the next time he acted on his rational beliefs about conflict.

Step 12: Generalize your learning

While you can really only deal with your emotional problem in specific situations, you can generalize what you have learned about dealing effectively with this unhealthy negative emotion across situations defined by the theme to which you are particularly vulnerable (e.g. hurting people's feelings), and you can also apply your learning to situations defined by a different theme with which you may have problems (e.g. being treated unfairly) when you are held responsible for or blamed for upsetting others.

John transferred his learning to other people who blamed him for upsetting them, and while conflict ensued with some of those with whom he asserted himself, this did not happen as much as John had previously predicted.

Other important issues in dealing with your target problem

In the above section, I outlined a 12-step programme to deal with your target problem about a theme related to being blamed for upsetting others. In this section, I will discuss some other important issues that may be relevant to you in your work to becoming less prone to this emotional problem. If you want to, you can incorporate them as additional steps in the above step-by-step guide at points relevant to you.

Why you overestimate the presence of the theme and how to deal with it

If you are prone to experiencing a particular unhealthy negative emotion, then you will be particularly sensitive to seeing the presence of the relevant theme at 'A', where others, who are not prone to the same emotion, do not. Here is how you come to overestimate the presence of the theme. Let me use the unhealthy negative emotion and its related theme of anxiety as an example. In doing so, I will discuss the case of John who I first introduced in Chapter 4 and whose experience I used to illustrate the 12 steps discussed above. You will recall that John was anxious about being blamed by people for upsetting them because of the conflict that would ensue between them. However, John's anxiety problem about conflict related to being held responsible for or blamed for upsetting people was general in nature.

Why you overestimate the presence of your theme

This is how you come to overestimate the presence of your theme in your area of vulnerability. I will illustrate this with reference to John's general irrational belief.

1 You take the theme of your general irrational belief.

   Conflict from the general irrational belief: 'I must not have conflict with someone I care for, and if I did I couldn't bear it.'

2 You construct a second general irrational belief that features uncertainty about the original threat theme.

'I must be certain that I won't get into conflict. I can't bear such uncertainty.'

3   You bring this second general irrational belief to situations where it is possible that you may, for example, get into conflict with people close to you, and you make (in John's case) a threat-related inference in the absence of certainty from the threat.

'Since I don't have certainty that I won't get into conflict with others, then I will get into conflict with them.'

4   You focus on this inference and bring a specific version of your original general irrational belief to this inference. For example:

Inference: 'I will get into conflict with my cousin.'
Specific irrational belief: 'I must not have conflict with my cousin and I could not bear it if I did.'

How to deal with overestimating the presence of your theme

In order to deal with overestimating the presence of your theme you need to take a number of steps, which I will illustrate again with reference to John.

• Construct general rational alternatives, both to your original (in this case) threat-focused general irrational belief – 'I would prefer not to have conflict with someone I care for, but that does not mean that it must not happen. If I did have conflict with someone, it would be difficult to tolerate, but I could bear it and it would be in my interests to do so' – and to your second uncertainty-focused general irrational belief – 'I would like to be certain that I won't get into conflict with others, but I don't need to know this. Not knowing is difficult to bear, but I can bear it and it's worth it to me to do so.'

• Question both sets of beliefs until you are able to see the rationality of the two general rational beliefs and the irrationality of the two general irrational beliefs and can commit to implementing the former.

• Bring your uncertainty-focused general rational belief to situations where it is possible that you may come into conflict with others close to you, and make an inference based on the data at hand.

'I am not certain whether or not I will get into conflict with people who blame me for upsetting them, so let's consider the evidence.'

If there is evidence indicating there is a good chance that you will get into conflict with a person close to you, then use a specific version of your general conflict rational belief to deal with this. For example:

Inference: 'I will get into conflict with my cousin.'
Specific rational belief: 'I don't want to get into conflict with my cousin, but that does not mean that I must not do so. If I did, it would be a struggle for me to put up with, but I could do so and it is in my interests to do so.'

How to examine the accuracy of your theme-related inference if necessary

If you are still unsure whether your inference is accurate or inaccurate, answer one or more of the following questions:

- How likely is it that the threat (in this case) happened (or might happen)?
- Would an objective jury agree that the threat actually happened or might happen? If not, what would the jury's verdict be?
- Did I view (am I viewing) the threat realistically? If not, how could I have viewed (can I view) it more realistically?
- If I asked someone I can trust to give me an objective opinion about the truth or falsity of my inference about the threat, what would the person say to me and why? How would this person encourage me to view the threat instead?
- If a friend had told me that he or she had faced (were facing or were about to face) the same situation as I faced and had made the same inference of threat, what would I say to him or her about the validity of this inference and why? How would I encourage the person to view the threat instead?

Deal with emotional problems about your target problem

My main purpose in writing this book is to consider the main emotional problems you may have when others blame you for upsetting them and to show you what you can do to address these emotional problems effectively and efficiently.

Not only do you disturb yourself when you are blamed for upsetting others, you may also disturb yourself about disturbing yourself! Now when you do this, this meta-disturbance (literally disturbance about disturbance) may well have a detrimental effect on the work you are doing to deal with your target problem. If this is the case, what can you do?

Assess your emotional problem about your target problem

The best way to assess your meta-emotional problem about your target problem is to use the 'ABC' framework that I have discussed in this book.

Assess 'C'

As with your target problem, start with 'C'. Ask yourself: 'How do I feel about being anxious?' (if anxiety is your target emotion). The most common meta-emotions in this context are: anxiety, depression, guilt, shame and unhealthy self-anger.

Assess 'A'

The next step is for you to assess 'A'. Remember that 'A' stands for adversity, in this case the aspect of your target emotion you are most disturbed about. For example, if you are anxious about being anxious, you may be most disturbed about the following 'A's:

- the emotional pain of feeling anxious;
- the sense of losing control when you are anxious;
- the belief that you have a personal weakness when you are anxious.

Assess 'B'

The next step is to identify the irrational beliefs that account for your unhealthy meta-emotion. These will be a rigid belief and one of the following three extreme beliefs: an awfulizing belief, a discomfort intolerance belief or a depreciation belief. You will also need to identify the rational belief alternatives to these irrational beliefs. Remember that these are a flexible belief and one of the following three non-extreme beliefs: a non-awfulizing belief, a discomfort tolerance belief or an acceptance belief.

Question your beliefs

You are now ready to question your beliefs. While there are a number of ways to do this, I suggest the following:

- Consider together your rigid belief and your flexible belief and ask yourself which of the two is realistic, logical and more helpful and which is unrealistic, illogical and more harmful. Provide plausible and persuasive arguments (see Appendix 2).
- Consider together your most relevant extreme and non-extreme beliefs and ask yourself the same questions as above. Again, provide plausible and persuasive arguments (see Appendices 3–5).

Work in this way until you are ready to commit yourself to strengthening your rational beliefs and to weakening your irrational beliefs.

Act and think in ways that are based on your rational beliefs

In order to internalize your rational beliefs concerning salient aspects of your target problem about which you have previously disturbed yourself, you need to act and think in ways that are based on these rational beliefs. You need to do this repeatedly over time until your feelings change. I refer you to Appendix 1 for constructive behaviours and realistic ways of thinking that are consistent with the rational beliefs that underpin the healthy negative emotions of concern, sadness, remorse, disappointment and healthy anger.

Develop and rehearse a healthy perspective on being blamed for upsetting others

After you have dealt with your emotional problems in response to others blaming you for upsetting them, then it is valuable to develop a healthy perspective on such events. This is like an over-arching philosophy that, if you strive to develop it, will serve as a protection against such disturbance. In my view such a perspective comprises a number of elements, which I will now discuss.

Develop an undisturbed philosophy about being blamed for upsetting others

In this chapter, I have shown you what you need to do to deal effectively with any specific emotional problems you may have about being blamed for upsetting people. It's also important for you to develop what may be termed an undisturbed philosophy towards being blamed for upsetting people and related aspects. This involves you showing yourself the following:

1 While you would prefer not to be blamed for upsetting people, you don't have to be exempt from being thus blamed.
2 While it is bad to be blamed for upsetting people, it is not the end of the world.
3 While it is a struggle to tolerate being blamed for upsetting people, it is not intolerable and it is worth it to you to do so.
4 While it is bad to be blamed for upsetting people it does not prove that you are a bad person. You are a fallible human being, and this does not change whether or not you have contributed to the upset feelings of others.

Accept that while you can't upset someone you may have contributed to that person's upset feelings

As I have already discussed in Chapter 1, you cannot upset someone. People upset themselves by holding a set of irrational beliefs about your behaviour towards them. However, what you have done may have contributed to their upset and it is important that you take responsibility for your behaviour in this respect.

Strive to understand but don't argue

Strive to understand what you may have done that has contributed to the other person's upset feelings without getting caught up in arguments about cause. While your behaviour may have contributed to the other person's disturbed feelings, it is equally likely that the person has made an inference about your behaviour that he (in this case) has evaluated with his irrational beliefs which underpin his unhealthy negative emotion.

If you understand the other person's emotion, it is possible to identify the theme of the inference that the person has made with respect to your behaviour. Thus, if the person has said you have made him anxious, then you know that it is very likely that he has found something in your behaviour threatening to him, since threat is the key inferential theme at 'A' in the 'ABC' framework when the person feels anxious at 'C'. I suggest that you refer to Table 4.1 (see p. 28) for the inferential themes associated with each unhealthy negative emotion that the other person may have blamed you for causing.

While you are trying to find out what inference the person may have made about your behaviour, it is important that you avoid getting caught up in arguments about who or what caused the other person's upset. This is why I suggest that you engage in this exploration when you are in a reasonably rational frame of mind. It is when you are still disturbing yourself about being blamed for causing the other person's disturbed feelings that arguments are most likely to ensue about the determinants of his or her feelings.

Say sorry

To my mind, there are two types of sorry that are relevant when talking to people who have blamed you for upsetting them: 'sorry for' and 'sorry that'. When you acknowledge that you have done something that has contributed to another person's upset and regret doing so, then you can be said to be sorry for your behaviour and your apology will make that clear (e.g. 'I am sorry for acting in a way that you found threatening'). However, when you do not acknowledge that you have done something that has contributed to the person's upset, but you understand that his disturbed reaction is based on the inference he made about your behaviour and the irrational beliefs he held about this inference, then you can be said to be sorry that he felt disturbed about what you did (e.g. 'I am sorry that you felt anxious about what I did'). In this way, you can have an honest non-defensive conversation with the other person about your behaviour and his reaction without having to challenge the other's contention that you have upset him.

If appropriate, teach the principle of emotional responsibility

At the right time, offer to teach the other person the principle of emotional responsibility if he is interested, but give him time to process it. In Chapter 1, I pointed out that when someone blames you for upsetting him he is not taking responsibility for creating his own emotions. Once you have discussed the episode where the person blamed you for upsetting him and you have come to some resolution, it might be worth offering to teach him the principle of emotional responsibility. If so, here is one way of doing so, known as the 'money model'. This is how John taught his cousin, Robin, the money model when they had resolved the issue that gave rise to John being blamed for upsetting his cousin.

John: OK, Robin. I'd like to teach you a model which explains the factors that account for people's emotional problems. Are you interested in learning about this explanation?
Robin: Yes, I am.
John: Good. Now there are four parts to this model. Here's part one. I want you to imagine that you have £10 in your pocket and that you believe the following: 'I would prefer to have a minimum of £11 on me at all times, but it's not essential that I do so. It would be bad to have less than my preferred £11, but it would not be the end of the world.' Now, if you really believed this, how would you feel about having only £10 when you want, but don't demand, a minimum of £11?
Robin: I'd feel concerned.
John: Right. Or you'd feel annoyed or disappointed. But you wouldn't kill yourself.
Robin: Certainly not.

John: Right. Now, here's part two of the model. This time you hold a different belief. You believe the following: 'I absolutely must have a minimum of £11 on me at all times. I must! I must! I must! And it would be the end of the world if I had less.' Now, with this belief you look in your pocket and again find that you have only £10. How would you feel this time about having £10 when you demand that you must have a minimum of £11?

Robin: I'd feel quite panicky.

John: That's exactly right. And note something really important. Faced with the same situation, different beliefs lead to different feelings. Now, the third part of the model. This time you still have the same belief as you did in the last scenario, namely, 'I absolutely must have a minimum of £11 on me at all times. I must! I must! I must! And it would be the end of the world if I had less.' This time, however, in checking the contents of your pocket you discover two £1 coins nestling under the £10 note. How would you feel about now having £12 when you believe that you have to have a minimum of £11 at all times?

Robin: I'd feel very relieved.

John: Right. Now, here is the fourth and final part of the model. With that same £12 in your pocket and that same belief – namely, 'I absolutely must have a minimum of £11 on me at all times. I must! I must! I must! And it would be the end of the world if I had less' – one thing would occur to you that would lead you to be panicky again. What do you think that might be?

Robin: Let me think . . . I believe that I must have a minimum of £11 at all times, I've got more than the minimum and yet I'm anxious. Oh, I see! I'm now saying, 'I must have a minimum of £13.'

John: No. You are sticking with the same belief as before, namely, 'I must have a minimum of £11 on me at all times. I *now* have £12 . . .'

Robin: Oh, I see . . . I *now* have the £12. Right, so I'm scared I might lose £2.

John: Or you might spend £2 or you might get mugged. Right. Now the point of this model is this. All humans, black or white, rich or poor, male or female, make themselves disturbed when they don't get what they believe they must get. And they are also vulnerable to making themselves disturbed when they do get what they believe they must get, because they could always lose it. But when humans stick rigorously (but not rigidly) to their flexible or non-dogmatic preferences and don't change these into musts, then they will feel healthily concerned when they don't have what they prefer and will be able to take constructive action under these conditions to attempt to prevent something undesirable happening in the future.

Once you have taught someone the principle of emotional responsibility, give him (in this case) time to digest it before discussing it with him. Remember that he doesn't have to accept the principle of emotional responsibility. It is useful here to remind yourself of the old adage: 'You can bring a horse to water, but you can't make it drink.'

In the next chapter, I will discuss how those people I introduced in Chapter 4 used the material I have presented in this chapter.

6

Case examples of responding healthily to being blamed for upsetting others

Introduction

In this chapter, I will discuss how the people we first met in Chapter 4 used the material in Chapter 5 (or in one case did not use it) to deal healthily with being blamed for upsetting someone. I discussed John in Chapter 5, so I refer you to that chapter for more information about how he overcame his non-ego anxiety.

Betty – a case of ego anxiety

You will recall that Betty regarded herself as a dutiful wife but considered that Vivienne, her mother-in-law, never gave her credit for this; indeed, she often felt upset with Betty's treatment of her son and held Betty responsible for her upset. Whenever Betty visited her in-laws, she felt anxious about being held responsible by her mother-in-law for upsetting her.

Betty felt anxious about visiting her in-laws because she held the following irrational belief: 'My mother-in-law must not blame me for upsetting her and if she does it proves that I am worthless.' Once she had identified her irrational belief, she questioned it and showed herself that her worth as a person was not diminished by being blamed by Vivienne for upsetting her. She used imagery techniques to rehearse her flexible and self-accepting beliefs and resolved to discuss this issue with her mother-in-law without drinking alcohol first.

Having learned to accept herself for being blamed by her mother-in-law for upsetting her, Betty decided to ask Vivienne what she found upsetting in her behaviour. It transpired that Vivienne had old-fashioned ideas about how a wife should treat her son and Betty did not live up to these expectations. Betty told Vivienne that she was sorry that Vivienne felt hurt and angry about Betty's treatment of her son, but that they had different ideas about the role of a wife. Betty invited Vivienne to agree to differ on this subject but the latter refused, taking the line that she was right and Betty was wrong. Betty did not depreciate herself for being thought in the wrong. She accepted that Vivienne had a right to be blinkered in her view, but this had no impact on the way that Betty chose to view herself. Betty agreed to visit her in-laws three times a year because she knew it was important to her husband. However, she no longer felt anxious about going because she was able to accept herself in the face of her mother-in-law's criticism and blame.

Melanie – a case of depression about losing someone's affection

You will recall from Chapter 4 that Melanie became depressed when her sister blamed Melanie for making her feel guilty. Melanie inferred that this meant she had lost her sister's affection and made herself depressed about this loss. Melanie made herself depressed about losing her sister's affection because she held the following irrational belief: 'I must not lose my sister's affection and I am unlovable because I have.' Melanie challenged this belief and saw that, far from being a requirement, her sister's affection was desirable to her but not something that she had to have at all costs. She also came to see that the loss of her sister's affection, no matter how important to her, was only one aspect of her life, and the presence or absence of this important aspect could not define her lovability. She came to see that she was still lovable even if her sister had withdrawn her affection from her.

As Melanie developed this rational belief, she came out of her depressed shell, and when she felt strong enough she asked her sister what she felt guilty about that led her to blame Melanie for creating these feelings. Her sister replied that she felt guilty because Melanie seemed always to do the right thing and she herself always seemed to do the wrong thing by comparison. Melanie empathized with her sister and said that she felt sorry that her sister felt this way, but that it was not her intention to make her sister feel anything. After they had talked the issue through, Melanie taught her sister the principle of emotional responsibility by going over the 'money model' with her (see pp. 61–3) and her sister found this helpful.

Melanie realized that she had a general tendency to infer the loss of another's affection even before the person had indicated that he or she blamed Melanie for upsetting his or her feelings. Melanie saw that she held not only a general irrational belief about the loss of affection (i.e. 'I must have the affection of those important to me and I am unlovable if I don't have affection') but also an uncertainty-related general irrational belief about affection (i.e. 'I must know that I have the affection of a person close to me and it is terrible not knowing this'). This latter belief led her to infer loss of affection if it was not clear that the person had affection for her. Melanie developed the following rational alternatives to both general irrational beliefs:

I would like to have the affection of those important to me, but I don't have to have it. I am not unlovable if I don't have the other's affection. I am still lovable whether or not I have it, although it is painful not to have it.

This general rational belief helped Melanie to feel sad but not depressed about losing affection, and encouraged her to stay in dialogue with the other person about the relevant incident rather than to withdraw into herself.

I would like to know I have the affection of a person close to me, but I don't need to know this. Not knowing this is unfortunate, but not terrible.

This general rational belief helped Melanie to infer loss of affection related to being blamed for upsetting someone only when it was clear that she had lost the person's affection.

Roger – a case of depression about failure
In Chapter 4, I mentioned Roger, who became depressed when his daughter blamed him for making her feel ashamed of her body. Roger inferred that this meant that he had failed as a father and made himself depressed about this failure because he held the rigid

belief: 'I must not fail as a father and I am a failure as a person if I do.' Roger questioned the demand part of this irrational belief and showed himself that regrettably there was no evidence to support his idea that he must not fail as a father. If there was, then he would not be able to fail. Also, this rigid belief led him to drink to excess, and when he was drunk it was much more likely that he would interact poorly with his daughter. He saw that his alternative flexible belief (i.e. 'I really don't want to fail as a father, but sadly it does not follow that I must not do so') was true, logical and healthier for him, since he did not drink to excess when he believed it and it helped him to have a rational discussion with his daughter. When he did so, she told him that what he thought was teasing she took as a criticism. Roger told his daughter that he was sorry that she took his teasing as criticism and resolved not to tease her again about the way she looked. She responded well to this and told him that in many other respects he was a great dad. This helped Roger to see that when he based his self-esteem on being a good dad in all respects then he was vulnerable to self-esteem problems when one of his children criticized his fathering skills. As he worked to develop self-acceptance, he took such criticisms in his stride, and when his children blamed him for making them feel upset he was sad about this, but saw it as something to explore and get to the bottom of rather than to escape from in a haze of alcohol.

Stella – a case of depression about an undeserved plight

You will remember Stella from Chapter 4. She became depressed when one of her students held her responsible for making him feel inadequate and made a formal complaint, which her college decided to investigate. Stella thought this was an undeserved plight and made herself depressed about it. She did so by believing: 'I must not be in this undeserved plight and it's terrible that I am. Poor me!'

In order to deal with her depressed feelings, Stella had to swallow a few bitter pills. She had to realize that while she did not deserve to be in the situation in which she found herself, it did not follow that she absolutely should not be in such a plight. It was unfortunate, unfair and uncomfortable, she reasoned, but not terrible. She also saw that she was not a 'poor' person; rather, she was a 'non-poor' person who was in a poor situation. This new rational belief system helped her to be sad about her plight rather than depressed about it, and helped her to stay focused when giving evidence to the investigative committee and not to ruminate on the issue. The committee established that the student felt inadequate when Stella gave him feedback, not about the content of his essay but about his spelling and punctuation. He argued that this was gratuitous feedback, meant to undermine him. The committee disagreed and ruled that it was entirely in order for a college lecturer to give feedback about style as well as content. They dismissed the case.

Susan – a case of guilt about doing the wrong thing

You may remember Susan, whose mother blamed her for making her (the mother) feel lonely. Susan inferred that this meant she had done the wrong thing by neglecting her mother and made herself guilty about this. Her guilt was based on the following irrational belief: 'I absolutely should not have done the wrong thing by neglecting my mother and I am a bad person for doing so.'

Susan helped herself by realizing that she was a fallible human being and not a bad person. Assuming temporarily that she had done the wrong thing by neglecting her mother, she challenged the idea that this wrongdoing could define her. If she was a bad person then all she could do would be bad things and this was hardly the case, she reasoned. Also, she argued, as a fallible human being she was not immune from acting badly and nor did she have to be immune. Holding this rational belief, Susan did not beg her mother to forgive her; rather, she engaged her mother in a discussion concerning her feelings of loneliness. While expressing sorrow for her mother's lonely feelings but not taking responsibility for them, Susan put it to her mother that she could help herself when she was lonely by calling on other people as well as Susan. Her mother immediately rejected this idea, but rather than argue about it Susan asked her mother to think about it. A few days later, her mother said, grudgingly, that Susan had a point!

Susan also came to see that she was prone to accepting others' views that she had done the wrong thing, even predicting this before it had happened. She identified the following general irrational belief that made her particularly prone to making inferences of wrongdoing: 'When I am involved, I must ensure that I do the right thing and that others see this too. If not, I have done the wrong thing and am a bad person for doing so.' Susan challenged this belief using the arguments outlined in Appendices 2 and 5, and developed this alternative general rational belief: 'When I am involved, I would like to ensure that I do the right thing and that others see this too, but it doesn't have to be this way. If not, then I may have done the right thing from one perspective even though others think I have done the wrong thing. If I have done the wrong thing, I am not a bad person, but a fallible human being capable of doing right and wrong.' Using this latter belief, Susan came to see that even if her immediate response was to think that she had done the wrong thing, she was able to stand back and use this rational belief to correct her immediate response. This helped her to see that she was overestimating the extent to which others blamed her for doing wrong, and that even when they did, they were using one perspective for doing so (e.g. 'It is Susan's job to put me first') and she could use a different one (e.g. 'If I don't put myself first nobody else will. I will help others when I can, but I will not put their well-being before my own').

As a result, Susan became far less prone to being manipulated through guilt by others, notably her mother.

Ben – a case of guilt about not doing the right thing

If you remember, Ben was invited to a party with a group of friends. Unbeknown to him, one of his friends, Martin, was not invited, something Ben only discovered when Martin did not show up at the party. When Martin found out that Ben and the others went to the party to which he was not invited, he felt hurt and blamed his friends for causing his hurt feelings. Ben responded to Martin's accusation with guilt. What Ben felt guilty about was that he did not do the right thing, which was to tell Martin about the invitation when he received it. His guilt was based on the following irrational belief: 'I absolutely should have done the right thing and told Martin about the party invitation and I am bad for not doing so.'

Ben challenged this belief by showing himself that even if he did not do the right thing, there was no absolute reason why he had to do the right thing. Indeed, he had made the assumption at the time that Martin had been invited and for some reason did not make it to the party. By demanding that he should have told Martin about the party, what Ben was effectively saying was that he absolutely should have thought differently at the time. While that would have been desirable, Ben came to see that to demand that he should not think what he was thinking was tantamount to him demanding that reality should not be reality when it was reality! Seeing this then helped Ben to accept himself as fallible rather than as being bad for not thinking to do at the time what he later discovered would have been the right thing.

Ben also saw that he had a tendency to define a situation the way someone close to him defined it when that person was upset. Thus, when Martin was upset he told Ben that the right thing would have been to tell him about the party. Ben agreed with this view, concluded that he had not done the right thing and then blamed himself for not doing it. However, when Ben developed the following rational belief: 'I wish I had done the right thing and told Martin about the party invitation, but there is no law of the universe decreeing that I absolutely should have done so. I am fallible for not doing so, not bad,' the remorse that he felt then enabled him to be more objective about whether or not he had failed to do the right thing. He concluded that according to the reasonable assumption he had made at the time – that Martin had been invited to the party and had for some reason failed to turn up – he had done the right thing by not doing anything. Only later, when it transpired that Martin had not been invited to the party and when Martin accused Ben of not doing the right thing, did it become clear what the right thing to do would have been. However, freed from the impact of his irrational belief, Ben saw that for him to have done what turned out to have been the right thing, he would have to have had fortune-telling powers.

Ben's rational belief helped him to face rather than avoid Martin. Ben told Martin that he was sorry that Martin was upset with him and explained that had he thought at the time what came to be the case later then he would have informed Martin about the party, and he would do so in future. However, Ben did not apologize for not doing the right thing because at the time he thought he had done the right thing. Somewhat grudgingly, Martin accepted Ben's position and they repaired their relationship.

Developing a flexible and self-accepting set of rational beliefs about not doing the right thing helped Ben to be far less prone to accepting in an uncritical way others' inferences that he had not done the right thing in situations. When he saw they were correct, he apologized for not doing the right thing (without self-blame), but he no longer assumed automatically that they were correct.

Loretta – a case of guilt about hurting someone's feelings

In Chapter 4 I introduced you to Loretta, who forgot to send her grandmother a birthday card and heard from her mother that her gran was very upset about this and held Loretta responsible for causing her hurt feelings. Loretta responded to this with guilt for hurting her gran's feelings. She did so because she held the following irrational belief: 'I absolutely should not have hurt my gran's feelings and I am bad for doing so.'

Loretta developed the following rational belief: 'I would have preferred not to have hurt my gran's feelings, but sadly that does not mean that I must not do so. I am not bad for doing so. I am a fallible human being who did the wrong thing.' If she had held this rational belief at the time, she would have phoned her gran to apologize but would not have overcompensated by buying her an 'over the top' gift as a way of begging forgiveness. Also, Loretta would have thought of people she had pleased as well as people she had hurt, rather than only of the people she had hurt, which was the case when she felt guilt.

This rational belief would have also helped Loretta to see that while her gran did feel hurt and that she had contributed to these feelings by forgetting to send a birthday card, it did not follow that Loretta had hurt her gran's feelings. Her gran's hurt feelings were based largely on her gran's own irrational beliefs about Loretta's failure to send the birthday card and not on Loretta's failure itself. All this helped Loretta not to dwell on the issue later. However, she also learned that it would be wise to keep a birthday list on her iPad for future reference.

Loretta applied all this learning to future occasions when others blamed her for upsetting them or she was told that they felt this way.

Brian – a case of shame about falling short of one's ideal

In Chapter 4, I introduced you to Brian, who felt ashamed when his girlfriend's father blamed Brian for making him angry when he discovered that, contrary to their agreement, Brian had kept his daughter out very late. Brian felt very ashamed about his actions, which he saw as evidence that he had fallen far short of what he expected of himself. His shame was based on the following irrational belief: 'I absolutely should have kept my agreement with my girlfriend's father and I am less of a person for not doing so.'

Brian dealt with his shame by showing himself that while it is important for him to achieve his ideal and keep to his agreement with his girlfriend's father, there is no law decreeing that he must not fall short of his ideal. Brian recognized that while his behaviour did not cause his girlfriend's father's anger, his actions had contributed to it. Holding a set of rational beliefs (i.e. 'I am not less of a person for falling short of my ideal. I am a fallible human being who wants to achieve his high standards, but does not always have to do so') allowed him to face both his girlfriend and her father and prompted him to apologize to the latter for not keeping to his agreement with him.

Mandira – a case of shame about letting down one's reference group

As I discussed in Chapter 4, Mandira came from a family who all got first-class degrees from Cambridge University. However, despite working very hard, Mandira was awarded an upper second rather than a first, and her family were very upset about what they regarded as her failure. They blamed Mandira for bringing shame to the family. Mandira responded to this by feeling ashamed about letting her family down because she held the following irrational belief: 'I absolutely should not have let my family down and I am defective for doing so.'

After she had run away from home, Mandira dealt with her shame in the following way. She recognized that if she was going to live her own life this meant that, given the belief system of most members of her family, they would feel ashamed about her actions. In that sense, she saw that rather than demanding that she must not let her family down, she could not help but let them down. She either let them down or let herself down, and she refused to do the latter. Of course, she would have preferred not to let her family down, but she realized that she was not exempt from doing so and nor did she have to be so exempt.

Mandira challenged the idea that letting her family down meant that she was defective as a human being. Instead, she saw herself as fallible and recognized that her identity could be defined neither by her family feeling let down by her actions nor by their shame.

Mandira grasped the idea that her actions did not directly lead to her family's shame. Rather, they felt shame because of their irrational belief system about her actions. When she saw a sympathetic aunt later, she told her that she felt sorry that most of her family felt shame, but she did not apologize for making them feel that way.

Mandira accepted, with much sadness, that if she chose to live her life then she would have no contact with most of her family members, at least for the foreseeable future.

Jeremy – a case of ego hurt about being accused unfairly of causing another's distress

Do you remember Jeremy from Chapter 4? He was a GP who prided himself on his good relationships with his patients. However, one day one of his patients made a complaint about him to the practice manager, stating that Jeremy had made her feel small by dismissing her concerns about her cough. Jeremy felt hurt about this because he thought that the accusation was unjustified and because he held the following irrational belief: 'My patient must not be unfair towards me, but I am less worthy for perhaps not doing enough for her.'

Jeremy dealt with his hurt feelings by showing himself that, despite his best efforts, there will always be patients who will make complaints, and this will happen whether it is fair or not. He accepted that he was not immune from this unfairness and that there was no law of the universe stating that he absolutely should be immune from it. He also saw that his worth as a person was not defined by his patients' responses to him – either positive or negative. All he could do was his best for everyone and accept that the old adage is probably true: 'You can't win them all.'

He still felt a sense of sorrow about the complaint, but did not recognize the behaviour that the patient in question had attributed to him when the practice manager spoke to her. The patient claimed that Jeremy had said, 'Don't waste my time, you silly woman. I have really sick people to see!' Jeremy knew that he hadn't said anything like that. In his response to this – and from a position of sorrow, not hurt – Jeremy said that he was sorry his patient felt the way she did, but he did not take responsibility for upsetting her. He strenuously denied saying what the patient claimed he said. It then transpired that the patient had left her previous GP practice because she felt belittled by the male GP there. The practice manager resolved that the patient would only see a female GP in future and promised to monitor the situation.

Lesley – a case of non-ego hurt about being accused unfairly of causing another's distress

In Chapter 4, I introduced you to Lesley, a woman who had always done a lot for her next-door neighbour, who had a hip problem and could not walk. Lesley would shop for her and generally run errands for the woman. One day, Lesley agreed to pick up her neighbour from a physiotherapy appointment, but was held up in traffic. When she finally arrived, she was told that her neighbour had ordered a taxi and had left.

When Lesley got home, she went next door to apologize and her neighbour was very upset with her, claiming that Lesley had made her angry by not picking her up. Lesley responded with hurt about this accusation, since she regarded it as unfair for two reasons: (1) the fact that her lateness in picking up her neighbour was out of her control, and (2) she had always helped out her neighbour whenever she could and considered that the latter had not taken any of this into account in her accusation. However, Lesley's hurt feelings stemmed from the following irrational belief: 'I must not be treated in such an unfair manner by my neighbour. I can't bear it. Poor me!'

Lesley dealt with her hurt feelings by swallowing a number of bitter pills:

- First, Lesley saw that no matter how well she treated her neighbour, it did not follow that her neighbour should not, in an absolute sense, treat her fairly, although this was, of course, undesirable.
- Second, Lesley saw that she could bear such unfairness, although she would never like it.
- Finally, Lesley disputed her 'poor me' attitude. Rather, she saw herself as a 'non-poor person' who was in a poor situation.

Her rational beliefs helped her to stop feeling hurt, although she was still sorrowful about it. She stopped sulking and went next door to talk things through with her neighbour. Her neighbour still blamed Lesley for making her angry, but Lesley was having none of it. She told her neighbour that she was only looking at it from her own perspective, and if she put herself in Lesley's shoes she would see that there was no way she could have avoided being late.

Also, Lesley told her neighbour that her anger was her own responsibility, and if she would care to apologize for her unfair accusation Lesley would be prepared to help her again. The next day, Lesley received a written apology from her neighbour and they began to repair their fractured relationship.

Harry – a case of unhealthy anger about another who has broken one's personal rule

Harry, who we first met in Chapter 4, believed strongly in the principle of emotional responsibility discussed in Chapter 1. When his sister held him responsible for making her feel hurt, he responded with unhealthy anger because he held the following irrational belief: 'My sister must take responsibility for her feelings and she is an idiot for not doing so.'

Harry challenged this irrational belief by showing himself that, while it would be better for all concerned if his sister took responsibility for her own feelings and did not blame him for causing them, unfortunately she did not have to do the right thing. Once he accepted this grim reality he gave up trying to convince her to take emotional responsibility. This helped him to listen to her point of view, and when he did that he discovered that she thought he had let her down by not phoning him to see how her daughter was after the latter had become ill. Harry could see that his failure to do that was wrong and may have contributed to her hurt feelings, and he told his sister that he was sorry he had not done so, without accepting that he was the cause of her feelings of hurt. This led them to repair the rift in their relationship, which they were not able to do when Harry was unhealthily angry about his sister's failure to take responsibility for her feelings and when he was trying to get her to take this responsibility without listening to her first.

Debbie – a case of unhealthy anger about another threatening one's self-esteem

Do you remember Debbie from Chapter 4? She was the woman who, on a visit to her uncle and aunt, broke a valuable vase. Her aunt was particularly upset and held Debbie responsible both for breaking the vase and for upsetting her. Debbie responded with unhealthy anger and left in a rage. Debbie's unhealthy anger was ego-defensive in nature and was based on the following irrational belief: 'My aunt absolutely should not have made me feel badly about myself and she is bad for doing so.'

Debbie helped herself in the following way, by recognizing that her real problem was her attitude towards herself. Rather than depreciate herself for breaking the vase and upsetting her aunt, she decided to accept herself for doing the wrong thing. This helped her to see that her aunt did not make her feel badly about herself and, indeed, she did not upset her aunt. She then wrote a letter to her aunt, apologizing for breaking the vase and for leaving angrily. However, she did not apologize for hurting her aunt's feelings.

Lawrence – a case of unhealthy self-anger about breaking one's own personal rule

As we saw from Chapter 4, it was important for Lawrence to have very good relationships with his family and friends. He was popular, but found it difficult to say 'no' to people who wanted to see him. As a result, he sometimes double-booked arrangements and had to let someone down at the last minute. When he did this to Gina, she was very upset and accused him of making her angry. Lawrence reacted to this by becoming unhealthily angry with himself, because he held the following irrational belief: 'I absolutely should not have broken my personal rule by upsetting Gina and I'm an unworthy person for doing so.'

All the people that I have mentioned in this chapter helped themselves by applying the steps and principles that I discussed in Chapter 5. However, this was not the case with Lawrence. He did nothing to help himself. He felt that he deserved to punish himself and therefore he maintained his unhealthy self-anger and the irrational beliefs that underpinned it.

Lawrence's case should serve as a reminder to you that you can help yourself deal healthily with being blamed for upsetting someone, but you need to work to do so. This particularly involves identifying and challenging your irrational beliefs, and developing and strengthening your rational beliefs by acting and thinking in ways consistent with them.

In the final chapter, I will bring together all the points that I have made in this book and offer a handy summary for you to use as an aide-memoire of what to do when you disturb yourself about being blamed for upsetting someone.

7

Putting it all together

The six principles

In this final chapter, I am going to pull everything together and remind you what you need to do when people blame you for upsetting them. In doing so, I will refer you back to the relevant chapters for a more extended discussion of the points covered. This chapter, then, will serve as a summary of what I have covered in the book, and it will also present new material on how best to discuss what happened in the episode in which the person blamed you for upsetting him or her. The chapter will take the form of six principles which, taken together, form a comprehensive approach to coping when people blame you for upsetting them. While I suggest that you familiarize yourself with all six principles, only use those that particularly apply to you or are relevant.

Principle 1: Un-disturb yourself about being blamed for upsetting someone

When someone blames you for upsetting him (in this case) and you disturb yourself about being blamed in this way, it is important that you un-disturb yourself before you talk to the person concerned. However, if you have meta-disturbance (i.e. you disturb yourself about your original disturbance) you may need to deal with this before your original disturbance, particularly if the presence of your meta-disturbance interferes with you working on your original disturbance.

Work on your meta-disturbance

If you have meta-disturbance, then it is important that you work on the irrational beliefs that underpin this meta-disturbance. Basically, you do this by showing yourself that while it is undesirable for you to disturb yourself about your disturbance, it does not follow that you must not do so. If you do, then work towards self-acceptance for doing so and tolerate the discomfort that is often associated with meta-disturbance.

When you have dealt effectively with your meta-disturbance, then you can focus on your original disturbance about being blamed for upsetting someone. When you do this, use the 12-step guide that I discussed fully in Chapter 5.

Use the 12-step guide to deal with your disturbance about being blamed for upsetting someone

Here is a summary of the 12-step guide:

Step 1:   Specify your emotional problems about being blamed for upsetting someone.

Step 2:   Select and deal with one emotional problem at a time.

Step 3:   Identify reasons why your target problem is a problem for you and why you want to change.

Step 4:   Take responsibility for your target emotional problem.

Step 5:   Identify the themes at 'A' about which you disturb yourself and assume temporarily that they are true.

Step 6:   Identify the three components of your disturbed response (i.e. emotional, behavioural and thinking) and set goals with respect to each component.

Step 7:   Identify your general irrational beliefs and alternative general rational beliefs.

Step 8:   Question your general beliefs.

Step 9:   Rehearse your rational beliefs while facing in your imagination situations reflecting your theme at 'A'.

Step 10: Face your theme in reality.

Step 11: Capitalize on what you have learned.

Step 12: Generalize your learning.

Understand why you overestimate the presence of the theme and deal with your overestimations

Once you have un-disturbed yourself about the theme or themes related to your being blamed for upsetting someone, you need to understand why you overestimate the presence of such themes and deal with this. This involves you identifying your general irrational belief and a related uncertainty-based general irrational belief. In particular, it is the latter that leads you to overestimate the presence of the theme. If you develop rational alternatives to these beliefs, this will help you to form more accurate theme-related inferences.

Principle 2: Remember the principle of emotional responsibility

You have now un-disturbed yourself about being blamed for upsetting someone and you are almost ready to talk to that person about being blamed. However, before you do so, it is important that you remind yourself of the principle of emotional responsibility as applied to you being blamed for upsetting someone. Keep in mind, therefore, when you are being blamed by the person for upsetting him, that in reality he has upset himself about something that you have done (or failed to do). However, don't try to persuade the other person to adopt this principle at this point. If you do, the other person will become defensive and resist your efforts.

Principle 3: Try to understand why you are being blamed and respond accordingly

In Chapter 3, I discussed six reasons why people blame you for upsetting them. I will present these reasons in outline form and will give brief suggestions concerning how to respond to the person in each category.

- People blame you for upsetting them because they do not know about the principle of emotional responsibility.

In this case, you might ask the person what he was upset about with respect to your behaviour and teach him the principle of emotional responsibility when it becomes clear that the only reason he blames you for upsetting him is that he does not know about this principle.

- People blame you for upsetting them because they have objections to the principle of emotional responsibility.

In this case, provide counters to the person's objections to the principle of emotional responsibility.

- People blame you for upsetting them to avoid blaming themselves for creating their disturbed feelings.

In this case, you need to help the person to see that he can accept himself for when he takes responsibility for creating his own upset.

- People blame you for upsetting them because they do not know how to change their disturbed feelings.

In this case you need to help the person see how he can change his disturbed feelings or refer him to a relevant source, if he is interested (e.g. my book for Sheldon Press (2012) entitled *Eight Deadly Emotions: What they are and how to deal with them*).

- People blame you for upsetting them to avoid working to change their disturbed feelings.

In this case, if the person wants to face up to and do the hard work to change his disturbed feelings, you might suggest that he considers reading my book for Sheldon Press (2009) entitled *Self-discipline: How to get it and how to keep it*.

- People blame you for upsetting them so that they can feel sorry for themselves.

Here, the person may benefit from talking to a counsellor who would help him to consider what benefits he derives from self-pity. However, since an attachment to self-pity involves being passive, please do not expect the person to act on your suggestion that he talk to a counsellor. It may be that there is nothing you can do or say to help the person surrender this attachment and, thus, that you must expect the person to continue to blame you for upsetting him. If this does happen, continue to un-disturb yourself about this.

Principle 4: Try to understand what you are being blamed for

In Chapter 2, I discussed the disturbed emotions others experience that they blame you for causing. If you are going to have a productive conversation about the relevant episode, it is important that you try to understand what you are being blamed for. This involves you thinking about the other person's experience using the 'ABC' framework. Of course, you are not doing therapy with the other person so you will not be concerned with his or her irrational beliefs. But you will need to understand what disturbed feelings the person experienced at 'C' and what inferences he or she made at 'A'. I suggest that you consult Table 7.1 for help here. In this table, I outline the eight unhealthy negative emotions that people experience when they blame you for upsetting them and what they are disturbed about when they experience these disturbed emotions.

As you try to understand what you are being blamed for, I suggest that you do the following.

Use questions to identify the person's upset

When a person says to you that you have upset him, the term 'upset' is rather vague. Try to find out which of the eight unhealthy negative emotions he actually felt. You can do this by asking specific questions about his 'upset'. Here are two suggestions:

What specific emotion did you feel when you felt upset with me?
What did you feel like doing when you felt upset with me?

By asking this question you can infer the person's emotion from his action tendencies (see Appendix 1 for the actions and action tendencies associated with unhealthy negative emotions).

As you talk to him you may get a sense of what specific form of upset he experienced in the episode under consideration. In this case, put forward your hunch and the person will either confirm or deny it. For example:

Table 7.1 The eight unhealthy negative emotions that people experience when they blame you for upsetting them, and what they are disturbed about when they experience these disturbed emotions

When other people feel disturbed about something you did and blame you for causing their upset:

They experience at 'C'	They are most disturbed at 'A' that . . .
Anxiety	• You have threatened their self-esteem or sense of comfort.
Depression	• They have lost your affection. • You have reminded them that they have failed in some way. • Your behaviour represents an undeserved plight for them.
Guilt	• You have reminded them that they have done something wrong. • You have reminded them that they have failed to do the right thing. • They think that they have hurt your feelings.
Shame	• You have reminded them that they have fallen very short of their ideal. • Your behaviour has let down the reference group to which you both belong.
Hurt	• You have treated them unfairly. • You think less of your relationship with them than they do.
Unhealthy anger at others	• You have broken one of their personal rules. • You have threatened their self-esteem.
at self	• You have reminded them that they have broken one of their own personal rules.
Unhealthy jealousy	• You pose a threat to the person's relationship with his or her partner. • A threat is posed by uncertainty the person faces concerning his or her partner's whereabouts, behaviour or thinking in the context of the first threat.
Unhealthy envy	• You possess and enjoy something that the other person desires, but does not have.

I get the impression as you talk that you felt hurt with me. Is that right?

If the person denies the hunch, he may tell you what specific emotion he experienced as he corrects you. For example: 'No, I wasn't hurt, I was very angry with you.'

As you use questions and engage the person in a conversation about his emotional experience that he blames you for causing, it is important that you neither legitimize nor contradict such blame. This means avoiding saying such things as: 'How did you feel when I upset you?' As you can see, this legitimizes the idea that you can, in effect, cause the other person's feelings. Instead, say such things as: 'How did you feel when you were upset with me?' Note that this latter question avoids making causal statements (i.e. it does not state 'I upset you'), but asserts a connection between your behaviour and his feelings. Thus, try to use connection statements and avoid using causal statements. There is one exception to the latter. Here you use a causal statement, but you make it clear that such cause is seen from the perspective of the other person. Here is an example of this:

How did you feel when, from your perspective, I upset you?

Note the importance of the phrase 'from your perspective'. Given its importance, you may want to give it some emphasis as you talk to the other person. However, don't give it so much emphasis that the person experiences it as a criticism.

How to identify what the person was upset about

When you come to ask the person what he was upset about, use the specific emotion that you have identified (if you have identified one) in your questions. So rather than say: 'What did I do that you found upsetting?' you could ask: 'When you were angry, from your perspective, what did I do that you were angry about?'

Let's look carefully at that question.

- It contains a specific emotion (anger).
- It stresses the other person's frame of reference ('from your perspective').

Table 7.2 Questions you can ask to discover why someone blamed you for upsetting him or her

These questions are informed by the inferential themes related to each disturbed emotion.

If the person blames you for making him or her feel	Ask
Anxious	• When you felt anxious, did I do something that you found threatening in some way?
Depressed	• When you felt depressed, did you think that you had lost my affection? • When you felt depressed, did I remind you that you had failed in some way? • When you felt depressed, did you respond to what I said or did as though you were in a situation that you didn't deserve?
Guilty	• When you felt guilty, did I remind you that you had done something wrong? • When you felt guilty, did I remind you that you had not done the right thing? • When you felt guilty did I remind you that you had hurt someone's feelings?
Shame	• When you felt ashamed, did I remind you that you had fallen far short of your ideal? • When you felt ashamed, did I remind you that you had let down the reference group to which you belong?
Hurt	• When you felt hurt, did you think that I had treated you unfairly in some way? • When you felt hurt, did you think that I valued our relationship less than you do?
Unhealthy anger at others	• When you felt angry with me, did I break one of your personal rules? • When you felt angry, did I threaten your self-esteem in some way?
Unhelathy anger at self	• When you felt angry with yourself, did I remind you that you had broken one of your own personal rules?
Unhealthy jealousy	• When you felt jealous, did I pose a threat to your relationship with your partner in some way?

	• When you felt jealous, did you find being uncertain about what was going on between me and your partner threatening in some way?
Unhealthy envy	• When you felt envious, did I remind you that I had something that you wanted, but did not have?

- You are not taking responsibility for causing the person's feelings ('What did I do that you were angry about?' rather than 'What did I do that made you angry?'). If you want to talk the person's language, make sure that you stress that it is his perspective (e.g. 'What did I do that, from your perspective, made you angry?').

Use emotion-related inference themes in your questioning

As Table 7.1 shows, when a person experiences an unhealthy negative emotion he (in this case) has disturbed himself about a particular adversity. When you are attempting to find out what the other person is blaming you for, you can use the particular theme of the emotion in your questioning (see Table 7.2).

Try to get the person to be descriptive and specific

When the person responds to your questions, try to get him to describe what you did that he found upsetting as specifically as possible. Continue in this way until you know specifically what he thought you did that he found upsetting.

Don't get caught up in arguments about 'A'

During this process, remember that your goal is to understand what the person has blamed you for in causing his upset. In doing so, you need to understand that person's experience from his perspective. Consequently, it is important that you do not argue with the person about the accuracy of his inferences at 'A'. For example, he may think that you criticized him and find this threatening. You may disagree with this, but it is important that you do not argue with him about his inference. If you do, he will become defensive and you are unlikely to come to a resolution when he is a defensive state of mind.

Principle 5: Respond to the person using the 'two sorry' technique, but give your perspective

If you know specifically what you have done that the other person found upsetting, then you can use what I call the 'two sorry' technique. As I discussed in Chapter 5, if you think that your behaviour did contribute to (but, of course, did not cause) the other person's upset, then say that you are sorry *for* acting in such a way that contributed towards his upset, but do not take responsibility for causing his upset. However, if you disagree with the other person's inference about your behaviour, then say that you are sorry *that* he felt the way he did, but do not say sorry for contributing to his upset.

The purpose of the 'two sorry' technique is to demonstrate empathy for the other person's experience without taking responsibility for causing his feelings and without admitting to behaviour that, from your perspective, you did not commit.

Give your perspective

Once the person has demonstrated that he has felt understood, you can offer your perspective on the episode, while validating his perspective if you have different views on events. Here is an example of what I mean:

> *I am sorry that you felt anxious about what, from your perspective, was my critical behaviour. From my perspective, I was trying to be helpful.*

Principle 6: Ask for feedback

You are now ready to ask for and receive feedback from the other person concerning your behaviour and how he or she would have preferred you to behave. Of course, you are not obligated to accept this feedback, but it is important to the other person that you show that you are open-minded enough to receive such feedback and to consider it.

Taking the above example, let me illustrate what I mean.

*OK, from my perspective, I was trying to be helpful, but from your per-
spective, you found me critical. What could I have done for you not to
find me critical?*

When the person has given you feedback, it is important that you
thank him or her and indicate that you will give serious consideration to what has been said. Thus:

Thank you for that feedback, I will give it some serious thought.

If you implement the six principles that I have outlined in this
chapter, it is my view that you will increase the chances of both
coping with being blamed for upsetting others and maintaining a
good relationship with these others. However, this does not mean
that these outcomes will definitely occur. It may be that nothing
you can do will dissuade the other person from blaming you for
upsetting him or her, and if this is the case you need to accept this
grim reality without disturbing yourself about it.

This brings us to the end of the book. I would be interested in
your experiences in using the material in this book to deal with
people who blame you for upsetting them. You may write to me c/o
Sheldon Press.

Appendix 1

Healthy vs unhealthy negative emotions

Anxiety vs concern

Adversity • You are facing a threat to your personal domain.

Belief   IRRATIONAL   RATIONAL

Emotion   Anxiety   Concern

Behaviour
• You avoid the threat.
• You withdraw physically from the threat.
• You ward off the threat (e.g. by rituals or superstitious behaviour).
• You try to neutralize the threat (e.g. by being nice to people of whom you are afraid).
• You distract yourself from the threat by engaging in other activity.
• You keep checking on the current status of the threat, hoping to find that it has disappeared or become benign.
• You seek reassurance from others that the threat is benign.
• You seek support from others so that if the threat happens they will handle it or be there to rescue you.
• You over-prepare in order to minimize the threat happening or so that you are prepared to meet it. (NB it is the over-preparation that is the problem here.)

• You face up to the threat without using any safety-seeking measures.
• You take constructive action to deal with the threat.
• You seek support from others to help you face up to the threat and then take constructive action by yourself rather than relying on them to handle it for you or to be there to rescue you.
• You prepare to meet the threat but do not over-prepare.

- You tranquillize your feelings so that you don't think about the threat.
- You overcompensate for feeling vulnerable by seeking out an even greater threat to prove to yourself that you can cope.

Subsequent thinking

Threat-exaggerating thinking

- You overestimate the probability of the threat occurring.
- You underestimate your ability to cope with the threat.
- You ruminate about the threat.
- You create an even more negative threat in your mind.
- You magnify the negative consequences of the threat and minimize its positive consequences.
- You have more task-irrelevant thoughts than in concern.

- You are realistic about the probability of the threat occurring.
- You view the threat realistically.
- You realistically appraise your ability to cope with the threat.
- You think about what to do concerning dealing with the threat constructively rather than ruminating about the threat.
- You have more task-relevant thoughts than in anxiety.

Safety-seeking thinking

- You withdraw mentally from the threat.
- You try to persuade yourself that the threat is not imminent and that you are 'imagining' it.
- You think in ways designed to reassure yourself that the threat is benign or, if not, that its consequences will be insignificant.
- You distract yourself from the threat, e.g. by focusing on mental scenes of safety and well-being.
- You over-prepare mentally in order to minimize the threat happening or so that you are

prepared to meet it (NB once again it is the over-preparation that is the problem here).

- You picture yourself dealing with the threat in a masterful way.
- You overcompensate for your feeling of vulnerability by picturing yourself dealing effectively with an even bigger threat.

Depression vs sadness

Adversity	• You have experienced a loss from the sociotropic and/or autonomous realms of your personal domain.	
	• You have experienced failure within the sociotropic and/or autonomous realms of your personal domain.	
	• You or others have experienced an undeserved plight.	

Belief	*IRRATIONAL*	*RATIONAL*
Emotion	*Depression*	*Sadness*
Behaviour	• You become over-dependent on and seek to cling to others (particularly in sociotropic depression).	• You seek out reinforcements after a period of mourning (particularly when your inferential theme is loss).
	• You bemoan your fate or that of others to anyone who will listen (particularly in pity-based depression).	• You create an environment inconsistent with depressed feelings.
	• You create an environment consistent with your depressed feelings.	• You express your feelings about the loss, failure or undeserved plight and talk in a non-complaining way about these feelings to significant others.
	• You attempt to terminate feelings of depression in self-destructive ways.	
Subsequent thinking	• You see only negative aspects of the loss, failure or undeserved plight.	• You are able to recognize both negative and positive aspects of the loss or failure.
	• You think of other losses, failures and undeserved plights that you (and in the case of the latter, others) have experienced.	• You think you are able to help yourself.
	• You think you are unable to help yourself (helplessness).	• You look to the future with hope.
	• You only see pain and blackness in the future (hopelessness).	
	• You see yourself being totally dependent on others (in autonomous depression).	

- You see yourself as being disconnected from others (in sociotropic depression).
- You see the world as full of undeservedness and unfairness (in plight-based depression).
- You tend to ruminate concerning the source of your depression and its consequences.

Guilt vs remorse

Adversity	• You have broken your moral code. • You have failed to live up to your moral code. • You have hurt someone's feelings.	
Belief	IRRATIONAL	RATIONAL
Emotion	Guilt	Remorse
Behaviour	• You escape from the unhealthy pain of guilt in self-defeating ways. • You beg forgiveness from the person you have wronged. • You promise unrealistically that you will not 'sin' again. • You punish yourself physically or by deprivation. • You defensively disclaim responsibility for wrongdoing. • You reject offers of forgiveness.	• You face up to the healthy pain that accompanies the realization that you have sinned. • You ask, but do not beg, for forgiveness. • You understand the reasons for your wrongdoing and act on your understanding. • You atone for the sin by taking a penalty. • You make appropriate amends. • You do not make excuses for your behaviour or enact other defensive behaviour. • You do accept offers of forgiveness.
Subsequent thinking	• You conclude that you have definitely committed the sin. • You assume more personal responsibility than the situation warrants. • You assign far less responsibility to others than is warranted. • You dismiss possible mitigating factors for your behaviour. • You only see your behaviour in a guilt-related context and fail to put it into an overall context. • You think that you will receive retribution.	• You take into account all relevant data when judging whether or not you have 'sinned'. • You assume an appropriate level of personal responsibility. • You assign an appropriate level of responsibility to others. • You take into account mitigating factors. • You put your behaviour into overall context. • You think you may be penalized rather than receive retribution.

Shame vs disappointment

Adversity	• Something highly negative has been revealed about you (or about a group with whom you identify) by yourself or by others.	
	• You have acted in a way that falls very short of your ideal.	
	• Others look down on or shun you (or a group with whom you identify) or you think that they do.	

Belief	IRRATIONAL	RATIONAL
Emotion	Shame	Disappointment
Behaviour	• You remove yourself from the 'gaze' of others.	• You continue to participate actively in social interaction.
	• You isolate yourself from others.	• You respond positively to attempts of others to restore social equilibrium.
	• You save face by attacking other(s) who have 'shamed' you.	
	• You defend your threatened self-esteem in self-defeating ways.	
	• You ignore attempts by others to restore social equilibrium.	
Subsequent thinking	• You overestimate the negativity of the information revealed.	• You see the information revealed in a compassionate self-accepting context.
	• You overestimate the likelihood that the judging group will notice or be interested in the information.	• You are realistic about the likelihood that the judging group will notice or be interested in the information revealed.
	• You overestimate the degree of disapproval you (or your reference group) will receive.	• You are realistic about the degree of disapproval you (or your reference group) will receive.
	• You overestimate how long any disapproval will last.	• You are realistic about how long any disapproval will last.

Hurt vs sorrow

Adversity	• Others treat you badly (and you think you do not deserve such treatment).
	• You think that the other person has devalued your relationship (i.e. someone indicates that his or her relationship with you is less important to him or her than the relationship is to you).

Belief	IRRATIONAL	RATIONAL
Emotion	Hurt	Sorrow
Behaviour	• You stop communicating with the other person.	• You communicate your feelings to the other directly.
	• You sulk and make it obvious you feel hurt without disclosing details of the matter.	• You request that the other person acts in a fairer manner towards you.
	• You indirectly criticize or punish the other person for his or her offence.	
Subsequent thinking	• You overestimate the unfairness of the other person's behaviour.	• You are realistic about the degree of unfairness in the other person's behaviour.
	• You think that the other person does not care for you or is indifferent to you.	• You think that the other person has acted badly rather than as demonstrating lack of caring or indifference.
	• You see yourself as alone, uncared for or misunderstood.	• You see yourself as being in a poor situation, but still connected to, cared for by and understood by others not directly involved in the situation.
	• You tend to think of past 'hurts'.	• If you think of past hurts you do so with less frequency and less intensity than when you feel hurt.
		• You are open to the idea of making the first move towards the other person.

Unhealthy anger vs healthy anger

Adversity
- You think that you have been frustrated in some way.
- Your movement towards an important goal has been obstructed in some way.
- Someone has transgressed one of your personal rules.
- You have transgressed one of your own personal rules.
- Someone or something has threatened your self-esteem.

Belief	IRRATIONAL	RATIONAL
Emotion	*Unhealthy anger*	*Healthy anger*
Behaviour	• You attack the other(s) physically. • You attack the other(s) verbally. • You attack the other(s) passive-aggressively. • You displace the attack on to • another person, animal or object. • You withdraw aggressively. • You recruit allies against the other(s).	• You assert yourself with the other(s). • You request, but do not demand, behavioural change from the other(s). • You express your feelings about the loss, failure or undeserved plight and talk in a non-complaining way about your feelings about these to significant others. • You leave an unsatisfactory situation non-aggressively after taking steps to deal with it.
Subsequent thinking	• You overestimate the extent to which the other(s) acted deliberately. • You see malicious intent in the motives of the other(s). • You see yourself as definitely right and the other(s) as definitely wrong. • You are unable to see the point of view of the other(s). • You plot to exact revenge. • You ruminate about the other's behaviour and imagine coming out on top.	• You think that the other(s) may have acted deliberately, but you also recognize that this may not have been the case. • You are able to see the point of view of the other(s). • You have fleeting, rather than sustained, thoughts of exacting revenge. • You think that other(s) may have had malicious intent in their motives, but you also recognize that this may not have been the case. • You think of yourself as probably rather than definitely right and the other(s) as probably rather than definitely wrong.

Unhealthy jealousy vs healthy jealousy

Adversity	• A threat is posed to your relationship with your partner from a third person. • A threat is posed by uncertainty you face concerning your partner's whereabouts, behaviour or thinking in the context of the first threat.	
Belief	IRRATIONAL	RATIONAL
Emotion	*Unhealthy jealousy*	*Healthy jealousy*
Behaviour	• You seek constant reassurance that you are loved. • You monitor the actions and feelings of your partner. • You search for evidence that your partner is involved with someone else. • You attempt to restrict the movements or activities of your partner. • You set tests which your partner has to pass. • You retaliate for your partner's presumed infidelity. • You sulk.	• You allow your partner to initiate expressing love for you without prompting him or her or seeking reassurance once he or she has done so. • You allow your partner freedom without monitoring his or her feelings, actions and whereabouts. • You allow your partner to show natural interest in members of the opposite sex without setting tests.
Subsequent thinking	• You exaggerate any threat to your relationship that does exist. • You think the loss of your relationship is imminent. • You misconstrue your partner's ordinary conversations with relevant others as having romantic or sexual connotations. • You construct visual images of your partner's infidelity. • If your partner admits to finding another person attractive, you think that he or she finds that person more attractive than you and that he or she will leave you for this other person.	• You tend not to exaggerate any threat to your relationship that does exist. • You do not misconstrue ordinary conversations between your partner and another man or woman. • You do not construct visual images of your partner's infidelity. • You accept that your partner will find others attractive but you do not see this as a threat.

Unhealthy envy vs healthy envy

Adversity	• Another person possesses and enjoys something desirable that you do not have.	
Belief	IRRATIONAL	RATIONAL
Emotion	Unhealthy envy	Healthy envy
Behaviour	• You disparage verbally the person who has the desired possession to others. • You disparage verbally the desired possession to others. • If you had the chance you would take away the desired possession from the other (either so that you would have it or so that the other was deprived of it). • If you had the chance you would spoil or destroy the desired possession so that the other person did not have it.	• You strive to obtain the desired possession if it is truly what you want.
Subsequent thinking	• You tend to denigrate in your mind the value of the desired possession and/or the person who possesses it. • You try to convince yourself that you are happy with your possessions (although you are not). • You think about how to acquire the desired possession regardless of its usefulness. • You think about how to deprive the other person of the desired possession. • You think about how to spoil or destroy the other's desired possession.	• You honestly admit to yourself that you desire the desired possession. • You are honest with yourself if you are not happy with your possessions, rather than defensively trying to convince yourself that you are happy with them when you are not. • You think about how to obtain the desired possession because you desire it for healthy reasons. • You can allow the other person to have and enjoy the desired possession without denigrating that person or the possession.

Appendix 2

Rigid vs flexible beliefs

Appendix 2 shows why rigid beliefs are false, illogical and have largely unhealthy consequences, while flexible beliefs are true, logical and have largely healthy consequences.

Rigid belief

A rigid belief is false
For such a demand to be true the demanded conditions would already have to exist when they do not. Or as soon as you make a demand then these demanded conditions would have to come into existence. Both positions are clearly false or inconsistent with reality.

A rigid belief is illogical
A rigid belief is based on the same desire as a flexible belief but is transformed as follows:
'I prefer that x happens (or does not happen) . . . and therefore this absolutely must (or must not) happen.'
The first ('I prefer that x happens (or does not happen)') is not rigid, but the second ('. . . and therefore this must (or must not) happen') is rigid. As such, a rigid belief is illogical since one cannot logically derive something rigid from something that is not rigid.

Flexible belief

A flexible belief is true
A flexible belief is true because its two component parts are true. You can prove that you have a particular desire and you can provide reasons why you want what you want. You can also prove that you do not have to get what you desire.

A flexible belief is logical
A flexible belief is logical since both parts are not rigid and thus the second component logically follows from the first. Thus, consider the following flexible belief:
'I prefer that x happens (or does not happen) . . . but this does not mean that it must (or must not) happen.'
The first component ('I prefer that x happens (or does not happen)') is not rigid and the second ('. . . but this does not mean that it must (or must not) happen') is also non-rigid. Thus, a flexible belief is logical because it is composed of two non-rigid parts connected together logically.

A rigid belief has largely unhealthy consequences
A rigid belief has largely unhealthy consequences because it tends to lead to unhealthy negative emotions, unconstructive behaviour and highly distorted and biased subsequent thinking when the person is facing an adversity.

A flexible belief has largely healthy consequences
A flexible belief has largely healthy consequences because it tends to lead to healthy negative emotions, constructive behaviour and realistic and balanced subsequent thinking when the person is facing an adversity.

Appendix 3

Awfulizing vs non-awfulizing beliefs

Appendix 3 shows why awfulizing beliefs are false, illogical and have largely unhealthy consequences and non-awfulizing beliefs are true, logical and have largely healthy consequences.

Awfulizing belief

An awfulizing belief is false
When you hold an awfulizing belief about your adversity, this belief is based on the following ideas:

1 Nothing could be worse.
2 The event in question is worse than 100 per cent bad.
3 No good could possibly come from this bad event.

All three ideas are patently false and thus your awfulizing belief is false.

An awfulizing belief is illogical
An awfulizing belief is based on the same evaluation of badness as a non-awfulizing belief, but is transformed as follows:

'It is bad if x happens (or does not happen) . . . and therefore it is awful if it does (or does not) happen.'

The first component ('It is bad if x happens (or does not happen . . .)') is non-extreme, but the second ('. . . and therefore it is awful if it does (or does not) happen') is extreme. As such, an awfulizing belief is illogical since one cannot logically derive something extreme from something that is non-extreme.

Non-awfulizing belief

A non-awfulizing belief is true
When you hold a non-awfulizing belief about your adversity. this belief is based on the following ideas:

1 Things could always be worse.
2 The event in question is less than 100 per cent bad.
3 Good could come from this bad event.

All three ideas are clearly true and thus your non-awfulizing belief is true.

A non-awfulizing belief is logical
A non-awfulizing belief is logical since both parts are non-rigid and thus the second component logically follows from the first. Thus, consider the following non-awfulizing belief:

'It is bad if x happens (or does not happen) . . . but it is not awful if x does (or does not) happen.'

The first component ('It is bad if x happens (or does not happen)') is non-extreme and the second ('. . . but it is not awful if it does (or does not) happen') is also non-extreme. Thus, a non-awfulizing belief is logical because it is composed of two non-extreme parts connected together logically.

An awfulizing belief has largely unhealthy consequences
An awfulizing belief has largely unhealthy consequences because it tends to lead to unhealthy negative emotions, unconstructive behaviour and highly distorted and biased subsequent thinking when the person is facing an adversity.

A non-awfulizing belief has largely healthy consequences
A non-awfulizing belief has largely healthy consequences because it tends to lead to healthy negative emotions, constructive behaviour and realistic and balanced subsequent thinking when the person is facing an adversity.

Appendix 4

Discomfort intolerance vs discomfort tolerance beliefs

Appendix 4 shows why discomfort intolerance beliefs are false, illogical and have largely unhealthy consequences and discomfort tolerance beliefs are true, logical and have largely healthy consequences.

Discomfort intolerance belief

A discomfort intolerance belief is false
When you hold a discomfort intolerance belief about your adversity, this belief is based on the following ideas, which are all false:

1 I will die or disintegrate if the discomfort continues to exist.
2 I will lose the capacity to experience happiness if the discomfort continues to exist.
3 Even if I could tolerate it, the discomfort is not worth tolerating.

All three ideas are patently false and thus your discomfort intolerance belief is false.

A discomfort intolerance belief is illogical
A discomfort intolerance belief is based on the same sense of struggle as a discomfort tolerance belief, but is transformed as follows:

'It would be difficult for me to tolerate it if x happened (or did not happen), and therefore it would be intolerable.'

The first component ('It would be

Discomfort tolerance belief

A discomfort tolerance belief is true
When you hold a discomfort tolerance belief about your adversity, this belief is based on the following ideas, which are all true:

1 I will struggle if the discomfort continues to exist, but I will neither die nor disintegrate.
2 I will not lose the capacity to experience happiness if the discomfort continues to exist, although this capacity will be temporarily diminished.
3 The discomfort is worth tolerating.

All three ideas are patently true and thus your discomfort tolerance belief is true.

A discomfort tolerance belief is logical
A discomfort tolerance belief is logical since both parts are non-extreme and thus the second component logically follows from the first. Thus, consider the following discomfort tolerance belief:

'It would be difficult for me to tolerate it if x happened (or did not happen), but it would not be intolerable (and it would be worth tolerating).'

difficult for me to tolerate it if x happened (or did not happen)') is non-extreme, but the second ('. . . and therefore it would be intolerable') is extreme. As such, a discomfort intolerance belief is illogical since one cannot logically derive something extreme from something that is non-extreme.

The first component ('It would be difficult for me to tolerate it if x happened (or did not happen)') is non-extreme and the second ('. . . but it would not be intolerable (and it would be worth tolerating)') is also non-extreme. Thus, a discomfort tolerance belief is logical because it is composed of two non-extreme parts connected together logically.

A discomfort intolerance belief has largely unhealthy consequences
A discomfort intolerance belief has largely unhealthy consequences because it tends to lead to unhealthy negative emotions, unconstructive behaviour and highly distorted and biased subsequent thinking when the person is facing an adversity.

A discomfort tolerance belief has largely healthy consequences
A discomfort tolerance belief has largely healthy consequences because it tends to lead to healthy negative emotions, constructive behaviour and realistic and balanced subsequent thinking when the person is facing an adversity.

Appendix 5

Depreciation vs acceptance beliefs

Appendix 5 shows why depreciation beliefs are false, illogical and have largely unhealthy consequences and acceptance beliefs are true, logical and have largely healthy consequences.

Depreciation belief

A depreciation belief is false
When you hold a depreciation belief in the face of your adversity, this belief is based on the following ideas, which are all false:

1 A person (self or other) or life can legitimately be given a single global rating that defines that person's or life's essence, and the worth of a person or of life is dependent upon conditions that change (e.g. my worth goes up when I do well and goes down when I don't do well).
2 A person or life can be rated on the basis of one of that person's or life's aspects.

Both of these ideas are patently false and thus your depreciation belief is false.

A depreciation belief is illogical
A depreciation belief is based on the idea that the whole of a person or of life can logically be defined by one of that person's or life's parts. Thus:

Acceptance belief

An acceptance belief is true
When you hold an acceptance belief in the face of your adversity, this belief is based on the following ideas, which are all true:

1 A person (self or other) or life cannot legitimately be given a single global rating that defines that person's or life's essence, and the worth of a person or of life, as far as it exists, is not dependent upon conditions that change (e.g. my worth stays the same whether or not I do well).
2 Discrete aspects of a person and life can be legitimately rated, but a person or life cannot be legitimately rated on the basis of these discrete aspects.

Both of these ideas are patently true and thus your acceptance belief is true.

An acceptance belief is logical
An acceptance belief is based on the idea that the whole of a person or of life cannot be defined by one or more of that person's or life's parts. Thus:

'X' is bad . . . and therefore I am bad.
This is known as the part–whole error, which is illogical.

'X' is bad, but this does not mean that I am bad, I am a fallible human being even though 'x' occurred.

Here the part–whole illogical error is avoided. Rather, it is held that the whole incorporates the part, which is logical.

A depreciation belief has largely unhealthy consequences
A depreciation belief has largely unhealthy consequences because it tends to lead to unhealthy negative emotions, unconstructive behaviour and highly distorted and biased subsequent thinking when the person is facing an adversity.

An acceptance belief has largely healthy consequences
An acceptance belief has largely healthy consequences because it tends to lead to healthy negative emotions, constructive behaviour and realistic and balanced subsequent thinking when the person is facing an adversity.

Index